SYSTEMATIC THEOLOGY

PAUL TILLICH

SYSTEMATIC THEOLOGY

2

Existence and the Christ

SCM PRESS LTD

334 02346 7

First published 1957
by The University of Chicago Press, Chicago 60637
First published in Great Britain 1957
by James Nisbet & Co Ltd
This edition first published 1978
by SCM Press Ltd
58 Bloomsbury Street London wc1
Second impression 1978

Typeset in the United States of America and
Printed and bound in Great Britain by
Redwood Burn Limited, Trowbridge & Esher

TO THE FACULTY OF
THE UNION THEOLOGICAL SEMINARY
NEW YORK

PREFACE

SO MANY have asked for and urged the speedy publication of the second volume of *Systematic Theology* that I am afraid that its actual appearance will be something of an anticlimax. It certainly will be a disappointment for those who expected that the second volume would contain the three remaining parts of the system. For some time I shared this expectation myself. But when I started the actual writing, it became obvious that such a project would delay the appearance of the book indefinitely and that the volume itself would grow to an unmanageable size. So I came to an agreement with the publisher that the third part of the system, "Existence and the Christ" should appear as the second volume, and that the fourth and fifth parts, "Life and the Spirit" and "History and the Kingdom of God," should follow—I hope in the not too distant future.

The problems discussed in this volume constitute the heart of every Christian theology—the concept of man's estrangement and the doctrine of the Christ. It is therefore justifiable that they be treated in a special volume in the center of the system. This volume is smaller than the first and the projected third one, but it contains the largest of the five parts of the system.

The content of this book, after many years of class lectures had prepared the way, was presented to the Theological Faculty of the University of Aberdeen, Scotland, as the first year's Gifford Lectures. The second year of the Gifford Lectures dealt with the fourth part of the system. The preparation of these lectures was a tremendous step toward the final formulation of the problems and their solutions. I want to express—for the first time in print—my deep gratitude for the honor and occasion which the Gifford lectureship presented me. Of course, a book is different from a series of lectures, especially if the book represents a part of a larger whole. The lectures had to be considerably enlarged and partly rewritten in the light of a critical rereading. But the basic ideas are unchanged. The publication of the second year's Gifford Lectures will follow in the third volume.

Here I want to say a word to the prospective critics of this volume.

I hope to receive much valuable criticism of the substance of my thought, as I did with the first volume and my smaller books. Whether or not I am able to agree with it, I gladly accept it as a valuable contribution to the continuous theological discussion between theologians and within each theologian. But I cannot accept criticism as valuable which merely insinuates that I have surrendered the substance of the Christian message because I have used a terminology which consciously deviates from the biblical or ecclesiastical language. Without such deviation, I would not have deemed it worthwhile to develop a theological system for our period.

My thanks go again to my friend who is now also my colleague, John Dillenberger, who this time, in collaboration with his wife Hilda, did the hard work of "Englishing" my style and who rephrased statements which otherwise might be obscure or difficult to understand. My appreciation also goes to Henry D. Brady, Jr., for reading the manuscript and suggesting certain stylistic changes. I also want to thank my secretary, Grace Cali Leonard, who worked indefatigably in typing and partially correcting my handwritten manuscript. Finally, my gratitude is expressed to the publisher who made possible the separate appearance of this volume.

The book is dedicated to the Theological Faculty of the Union Theological Seminary. This is justified not only by the fact that the seminary received me when I came as a German refugee in 1933; not only by the occasions which the faculty and administration abundantly gave me for teaching, writing, and, above all, learning; not only by the extremely friendly co-operation throughout more than twenty-two years of academic and personal contacts, but also because the content of this volume was a center of theological discussion with students and faculty during all those years. Those who participated in these discussions will recognize their influence on the formulations of this book.

TABLE OF CONTENTS

INTRODUCTION

PART III. EXISTENCE AND THE CHRIST

INDEX

INTRODUCTION

INTRODUCTION

A. THE RELATION OF THE SECOND VOLUME OF *SYSTEMATIC THEOLOGY* TO THE FIRST VOLUME AND TO THE SYSTEM AS A WHOLE

A SYSTEM demands consistency, but one might well ask whether two volumes written seven years apart can be consistent with each other. If the systematic structure of the content is unchanged, they can be, even though the solutions to the special problems may differ. The many criticisms that have come and the new thoughts that have been developed in the interval have not changed the basic structure of the system. But they have certainly influenced the form and content in many respects. If the theological system were deductive, like a system in mathematics in which one assertion is derived from the other with rational necessity, changes in conception of thought would be damaging to the whole. Theology, however, does not have this character, and the present system is formulated in a way which expressly avoids this danger. After the central theological answer is given to any question, there is always a return to the existential question as the context in which a theological answer is again given. Consequently, new answers to new or old questions do not necessarily disrupt the unity between the earlier and later parts of the system. It is a dynamic unity, open for new insights, even after the whole has been formulated.

The third part of the system, covered in this second volume, clearly shows this characteristic. While the title of the second part of the system, "Being and God," is followed in this volume by that of "Existence and the Christ," there is no logically necessary or deductive step from being to existence or from God to the Christ. The way from essence to existence is "irrational"; the way from God to the Christ is "paradoxical." The exact meaning of these terms will be discussed later; at this point they only confirm the open character of the present system.

The transition from essential to existential being cannot be understood in terms of necessity. But, in the view of classical theology and of all the philosophers, artists, and writers who seriously look at the conflicts of man's existential situation, reality involves that step. Hence the jump

3

from the first to the second volume mirrors the leap from man's essential nature to its distortion in existence. But, in order to understand any distortion, one must know its undistorted or essential character. Therefore, the estrangement of existence (and the ambiguity of life) as delineated in this volume can be understood only if one knows the nature of finitude as developed in the first volume in the part on "Being and God." Further, in order to understand the answers given to the questions implied in estrangement and ambiguity, one must know not only the answer given to the question implied in finitude but also the theological method by which question and answer are related to each other. This does not mean that an intelligent reading of the second volume is entirely dependent upon reading the first; for, as has been indicated, in every part of the system the questions are developed anew and the answers related to them in a special way. Such independent reading of this volume will also be facilitated by a partial recapitulation and by a reformulation of ideas discussed in the first volume.

The fourth part of the system, "Life and the Spirit," will follow the third part, "Existence and the Christ," as the description of the concrete unity of essential finitude and existential estrangement in the ambiguities of life. The answer to be given in this part is the divine Spirit. But this answer is incomplete. Life remains ambiguous as long as there is life. The question implied in the ambiguities of life drives to a new question, namely, that of the direction in which life moves. This is the question of history. Systematically speaking, history, characterized as it is by its direction toward the future, is the dynamic quality of life. Therefore, the "riddle of history" is a part of the problem of life. But for all practical purposes it is useful to separate the discussion of history from the discussion of life generally and to relate the final answer, "eternal life," to the ambiguities and questions implied in man's historical existence. For these reasons a fifth part, entitled "History and the Kingdom of God," is added, even though, strictly speaking, this material belongs to categories of life. This decision is analogous to the practical reasons which dictated a first part, "Reason and Revelation," the material of which, systematically speaking, belongs to all the other parts. This decision also shows again the non-deductive character of the entire project. While there are disadvantages with respect to systematic strictness, the practical advantages are paramount.

The inclusion of the non-systematic elements in the system results in an interdependence of all parts and of all three volumes. The second volume not only is dependent on the first but makes possible a fuller understanding of it. In the earlier parts there are many unavoidable anticipations of problems which are fully discussed only in the later ones. A system has circular character, just as do the organic processes of life. Those who stand within the circle of the Christian life will have no difficulty in understanding this. Those who feel like strangers in this respect may find the non-systematic elements in the presentation somewhat confusing. In any case, "non-systematic" does not mean inconsistent; it only means non-deductive. And life is non-deductive in all its creativity and eventfulness.

B. RESTATEMENTS OF ANSWERS GIVEN IN VOLUME I

1. Beyond Naturalism and Supranaturalism

The rest of this section will be devoted to a restatement and partial reformulation of those concepts of the first volume which are especially basic to the ideas to be developed in the second. It would be unnecessary to do so if one could simply refer to what has been said in the earlier parts. This is not possible because questions have arisen in public and private discussions which must be answered first. In none of these cases has the substance of my earlier thought changed, but formulations have proved to be inadequate in clarity, elaboration, and emphasis.

Much criticism has been made concerning the doctrine of God as developed in the second part of the system, "Being and God." Since the idea of God is the foundation and the center of every theological thought, this criticism is most important and welcome. For many, the stumbling block was the use of the term "Being" in relation to God, especially in the statement that the first thing we must say about God is that he is being-itself or being as being. Before speaking directly on this issue, I want to explain in a different terminology the basic intention of my doctrine of God. This is more simply expressed in the title of this section: "Beyond Naturalism and Supranaturalism." An idea of God which overcomes the conflict of naturalism and supranaturalism could be called "self-transcendent" or "ecstatic." In order to make this (tentative and preliminary) choice of words understandable, we may distinguish three ways of interpreting the meaning of the term "God."

The first one separates God as a being, the highest being, from all other beings, alongside and above which he has his existence. In this position he has brought the universe into being at a certain moment (five thousand or five billion years ago), governs it according to a plan, directs it toward an end, interferes with its ordinary processes in order to overcome resistance and to fulfil his purpose, and will bring it to consummation in a final catastrophe. Within this framework the whole divine-human drama is to be seen. Certainly this is a primitive form of supranaturalism, but a form which is more decisive for the religious life and its symbolic expression than any theological refinement of this position.

The main argument against it is that it transforms the infinity of God into a finiteness which is merely an extension of the categories of finitude. This is done in respect to space by establishing a supranatural divine world alongside the natural human world; in respect to time by determining a beginning and an end of God's creativity; in respect to causality by making God a cause alongside other causes; in respect to substance by attributing individual substance to him. Against this kind of supranaturalism the arguments of naturalism are valid and, as such, represent the true concern of religion, the infinity of the infinite, and the inviolability of the created structures of the finite. Theology must accept the antisupranatural criticism of naturalism.

The second way of interpreting the meaning of the term "God" identifies God with the universe, with its essence or with special powers within it. God is the name for the power and meaning of reality. He is not identified with the totality of things. No myth or philosophy has ever asserted such an absurdity. But he is a symbol of the unity, harmony, and power of being; he is the dynamic and creative center of reality. The phrase *deus sive natura,* used by people like Scotus Erigena and Spinoza, does not say that God is identical with nature but that he is identical with the *natura naturans,* the creative nature, the creative ground of all natural objects. In modern naturalism the religious quality of these affirmations has almost disappeared, especially among philosophizing scientists who understand nature in terms of materialism and mechanism. In philosophy proper, in so far as it became positivistic and pragmatistic, such assertions about nature as a whole were required. In so far as a whole philosophy of life involving dynamic processes developed, it again approached the religious forms of naturalism.

The main argument against naturalism in whatever form is that it denies the infinite distance between the whole of finite things and their infinite ground, with the consequence that the term "God" becomes interchangeable with the term "universe" and therefore is semantically superfluous. This semantic situation reveals the failure of naturalism to understand a decisive element in the experience of the holy, namely, the distance between finite man, on the one hand, and the holy in its numerous manifestations, on the other. For this, naturalism cannot account.

This criticism of the supranaturalistic and the naturalistic interpretations of the meaning of "God" calls for a third way which will liberate the discussion from the oscillation between two insufficient and religiously dangerous solutions. Such a third way is not new.

Theologians like Augustine, Thomas, Luther, Zwingli, Calvin, and Schleiermacher have grasped it, although in a restricted form. It agrees with the naturalistic view by asserting that God would not be God if he were not the creative ground of everything that has being, that, in fact, he is the infinite and unconditional power of being or, in the most radical abstraction, that he is being-itself. In this respect God is neither alongside things nor even "above" them; he is nearer to them than they are to themselves. He is their creative ground, here and now, always and everywhere.

Up to this point, the third view could be accepted by some forms of naturalism. But then the ways part. At this point the terms "self-transcendent" and "ecstatic," which I use for the third way of understanding the term "God," become meaningful. The term "self-transcendent" has two elements: "transcending" and "self." God as the ground of being infinitely transcends that of which he is the ground. He stands *against* the world, in so far as the world stands against him, and he stands *for* the world, thereby causing it to stand for him. This mutual freedom from each other and for each other is the only meaningful sense in which the "supra" in "supranaturalism" can be used. Only in this sense can we speak of "transcendent" with respect to the relation of God and the world. To call God transcendent in this sense does not mean that one must establish a "superworld" of divine objects. It does mean that, within itself, the finite world points beyond itself. In other words, it is self-transcendent.

Now the need for the syllable "self" in "self-transcendent" has also become understandable: the one reality which we encounter is experienced in different dimensions which point to one another. The finitude of the finite points to the infinity of the infinite. It goes beyond itself in order to return to itself in a new dimension. This is what "self-transcendence" means. In terms of immediate experience it is the encounter with the holy, an encounter which has an ecstatic character. The term "ecstatic" in the phrase "ecstatic idea of God" points to the experience of the holy as transcending ordinary experience without removing it. Ecstasy as a state of mind is the exact correlate to self-transcendence as the state of reality. Such an understanding of the idea of God is neither naturalistic nor supranaturalistic. It underlies the whole of the present theological system.

If, on the basis of this idea of God, we ask: "What does it mean that God, the ground of everything that is, can stand against the world and for the world?" we must refer to that quality of the world which expresses itself in finite freedom, the quality we experience within ourselves. The traditional discussion between the naturalistic and the supranaturalistic ideas of God uses the prepositions "in" and "above," respectively. Both are taken from the spatial realm and therefore are unable to express the true relation between God and the world—which certainly is not spatial. The self-transcendent idea of God replaces the spatial imagery—at least for theological thought—by the concept of finite freedom. The divine transcendence is identical with the freedom of the created to turn away from the essential unity with the creative ground of its being. Such freedom presupposes two qualities of the created: first, that it is substantially independent of the divine ground; second, that it remains in substantial unity with it. Without the latter unity, the creature would be without the power of being. It is the quality of finite freedom within the created which makes pantheism impossible and not the notion of a highest being alongside the world, whether his relation to the world is described in deistic or theistic terms.

The consequences of the self-transcendent idea of God for concepts like revelation and miracle (which are decisive for the christological problem) have been fully developed in the part entitled "Reason and Revelation." These do not need restatement, but they do show the far-reaching significance of the ecstatic interpretation of the relation between God and the world.

However, there is one problem which has moved into the center of the philosophical interest in religion since the appearance of the first volume. This is the problem of the symbolic knowledge of God. If God as the ground of being infinitely transcends everything that is, two consequences follow: first, whatever one knows about a finite thing one knows about God, because it is rooted in him as its ground; second, anything one knows about a finite thing cannot be applied to God, because he is, as has been said, "quite other" or, as could be said, "ecstatically transcendent." The unity of these two divergent consequences is the analogous or symbolic knowledge of God. A religious symbol uses the material of ordinary experience in speaking of God, but in such a way that the ordinary meaning of the material used is both affirmed and denied. Every religious symbol negates itself in its literal meaning, but it affirms itself in its self-transcending meaning. It is not a sign pointing to something with which it has no inner relationship. It represents the power and meaning of what is symbolized through participation. The symbol participates in the reality which is symbolized. Therefore, one should never say "only a symbol." This is to confuse symbol with sign. Thus it follows that everything religion has to say about God, including his qualities, actions, and manifestations, has a symbolic character and that the meaning of "God" is completely missed if one takes the symbolic language literally.

But, after this has been stated, the question arises (and has arisen in public discussion) as to whether there is a point at which a non-symbolic assertion about God must be made. There is such a point, namely, the statement that everything we say about God is symbolic. Such a statement is an assertion about God which itself is not symbolic. Otherwise we would fall into a circular argument. On the other hand, if we make *one* non-symbolic assertion about God, his ecstatic-transcendent character seems to be endangered. This dialectical difficulty is a mirror of the human situation with respect to the divine ground of being. Although man is actually separated from the infinite, he could not be aware of it if he did not participate in it potentially. This is expressed in the state of being ultimately concerned, a state which is universally human, whatever the content of the concern may be. This is the point at which we must speak non-symbolically about God, but in terms of a quest for him. In the moment, however, in which we describe the character of this point or in which we try to formulate that for which we ask, a combination of symbolic with non-symbolic elements occurs.

If we say that God is the infinite, or the unconditional, or being-itself, we speak rationally and ecstatically at the same time. These terms precisely designate the boundary line at which both the symbolic and the non-symbolic coincide. Up to this point every statement is non-symbolic (in the sense of religious symbol). Beyond this point every statement is symbolic (in the sense of religious symbol). The point itself is both non-symbolic and symbolic. This dialectical situation is the conceptual expression of man's existential situation. It is the condition for man's religious existence and for his ability to receive revelation. It is another side of the self-transcendent or ecstatic idea of God, beyond naturalism and supranaturalism.

2. THE USE OF THE CONCEPT OF BEING IN SYSTEMATIC THEOLOGY

When a doctrine of God is initiated by defining God as being-itself, the philosophical concept of being is introduced into systematic theology. This was so in the earliest period of Christian theology and has been so in the whole history of Christian thought. It appears in the present system in three places: in the doctrine of God, where God is called being as being or the ground and the power of being; in the doctrine of man, where the distinction is carried through between man's essential and his existential being; and, finally, in the doctrine of the Christ, where he is called the manifestation of the New Being, the actualization of which is the work of the divine Spirit.

In spite of the fact that classical theology has always used the concept of "being," the term has been criticized from the standpoint of nominalistic philosophy and that of personalistic theology. Considering the prominent role which the concept plays in the system, it is necessary to reply to the criticisms and at the same time to clarify the way in which the term is used in its different applications.

The criticism of the nominalists and their positivistic descendants to the present day is based on the assumption that the concept of being represents the highest possible abstraction. It is understood as the genus to which all other genera are subordinated with respect to universality and with respect to the degree of abstraction. If this were the way in which the concept of being is reached, nominalism could interpret it as it interprets all universals, namely, as communicative notions which point to particulars but have no reality of their own. Only the completely particular, the thing here and now, has reality. Universals are means of communication without any power of being. Being as such, therefore, does not designate anything real. God, if he exists, exists as a particular and could be called the most individual of all beings.

The answer to this argument is that the concept of being does not have the character that nominalism attributed to it. It is not the highest abstraction, although it demands the ability of radical abstraction. It is the expression of the experience of being over against non-being. Therefore, it can be described as the power of being which resists non-being. For this reason, the medieval philosophers called being the basic *transcendentale,* beyond the universal and the particular. In this sense the notion of being was understood alike by such people as Parmenides in Greece and Shankara in India. In this sense its significance has been rediscovered by contemporary existentialists, such as Heidegger and Marcel. This idea of being lies beyond the conflict of nominalism and realism. The same word, the emptiest of all concepts when taken as an abstraction, becomes the most meaningful of all concepts when it is understood as the power of being in everything that has being.

No philosophy can suppress the notion of being in this latter sense. It can be hidden under presuppositions and reductive formulas, but it nevertheless underlies the basic concepts of philosophizing. For "being" remains the content, the mystery, and the eternal *aporia* of thinking. No theology can suppress the notion of being as the power of being. One cannot separate them. In the moment in which one says that God *is* or that he has being, the question arises as to how his relation to being is understood. The only possible answer seems to be that God is being-itself, in the sense of the power of being or the power to conquer non-being.

The main argument of personalistic theology against the use of the concept of being is derived from the personalism of man's experience of the holy as expressed in the personal figures of the gods and the person-to-person relation of man to God in living piety. This personalism is most pronounced in biblical religion. In contrast to many Asiatic religions and to Christian mysticism, the question of being is not asked. For an extensive discussion of this problem I refer to my little book *Biblical Religion and the Search for Ultimate Reality* (Chicago: University of Chicago Press, 1955). The radical contrast of biblical personalism and philosophical ontology is elaborated without compromise. And it is emphasized that no ontological search can be found in the biblical literature. At the same time, the necessity to ask the ontological question is taken with equal seriousness. There is no ontological thought in biblical religion; but there is no symbol or no theological concept in it which does not have ontological implications. Only artificial barriers can stop the searching mind from asking the question of the being of God, of the gap between man's essential and existential being, of the New Being in the Christ.

For some, it is mostly the impersonal sound of the word "being" which produces concern. But suprapersonal is not impersonal; and I would ask those who are afraid to transcend the personalistic symbolism of the religious language to think, even if only for a short moment, of the words of Jesus about the hairs on our head being counted—and, we could add, the atoms and electrons constituting the universe. In such a statement there is at least as much potential ontology as there is actual ontology in the whole system of Spinoza. To prohibit the transformation of the potential into an actual ontology—of course, within the theological circle—would reduce theology to a repetition and organization of biblical passages. It would be impossible to call the Christ "the Logos."

In the last chapter of my book *The Courage To Be* (New Haven: Yale University Press, 1952) I have written of the God above the God of theism. This has been misunderstood as a dogmatic statement of a pantheistic or mystical character. First of all, it is not a dogmatic, but an apologetic, statement. It takes seriously the radical doubt experienced by many people. It gives one the courage of self-affirmation even in the extreme state of radical doubt. In such a state the God of both religious and theological language disappears. But something remains, namely, the seriousness of that doubt in which meaning within meaninglessness is affirmed. The source of this affirmation of meaning within meaninglessness, of certitude within doubt, is not the God of traditional theism but the "God above God," the power of being, which works through those who have no name for it, not even the name God. This is the answer to those who ask for a message in the nothingness of their situation and at the end of their courage to be. But such an extreme point is not a space within which one can live. The dialectics of an extreme situation are a criterion of truth but not the basis on which a whole structure of truth can be built.

3. Independence and Interdependence of Existential Questions and Theological Answers

The method used in the theological system and described in the methodological introduction of the first volume is called the "method of correlation," namely, the correlation between existential questions and theological answers. "Correlation," a word with several meanings in scientific language, is understood as "interdependence of two independent factors." It is not understood in the logical sense of quantitative or qualitative co-ordination of elements without causal relation, but it is understood as a unity of the dependence and independence of two factors. Since this kind of relation has become an object of discussion, I want to try to give some clarification concerning the independence and interdependence of existential questions and theological answers in the method of correlation.

In this method, question and answer are independent of each other, since it is impossible to derive the answer from the question or the question from the answer. The existential question, namely, man himself in the conflicts of his existential situation, is not the source for the revelatory answer formulated by theology. One cannot derive the divine self-manifestation from an analysis of the human predicament. God speaks to the human situation, against it, and for it. Theological supranaturalism, as represented, for example, by contemporary neo-orthodox theology, is right in asserting the inability of man to reach God under his own power. Man is the question, not the answer. It is equally wrong to derive the question implied in human existence from the revelatory answer. This is impossible because the revelatory answer is meaningless if there is no question to which it is the answer. Man cannot receive an answer to a question he has not asked. (This is, by the way, a decisive principle of religious education.) Any such answer would be foolishness for him, an understandable combination of words —as so much preaching is—but not a revelatory experience. The question, asked by man, is man himself. He asks it, whether or not he is vocal about it. He cannot avoid asking it, because his very being is the question of his existence. In asking it, he is alone with himself. He asks "out of the depth," and this depth is he himself.

The truth of naturalism is that it insists on the human character of the existential question. Man as man knows the question of God. He is estranged, but not cut off, from God. This is the foundation for the limited right of what traditionally was called "natural theology." Natural theology was meaningful to the extent that it gave an analysis of the human situation and the question of God implied in it. One side of the traditional arguments for the existence of God usually does this, in so far as they elucidate the dependent, transitory, and relational nature of finite human existence. But, in developing the other side of these arguments, natural theology tried to derive theological affirmations from the analysis of man's finitude. This, however, is an impossible task. None of the conclusions which argue for the existence of God is valid. Their validity extends as far as the questioning analysis, not beyond it. For God is manifest only through God. Existential questions and theological answers are independent of each other; this is the first statement implied in the method of correlation.

The second and more difficult problem is that of the mutual dependence of questions and answers. Correlation means that while in some respects questions and answers are independent, they are dependent in other respects. This problem was always present in classical theology (in scholasticism as well as in Protestant orthodoxy) when the influence of the substructure of natural theology upon the superstructure of revealed theology, and vice versa, was discussed. Since Schleiermacher, it has also been present whenever a philosophy of religion was used as an entering door into the theological system, and the problem arose of how far the door determines the structure of the house, or the house the door. Even the antimetaphysical Ritschlians did not escape this necessity. And the famous "No" of Karl Barth against any kind of natural theology, even of man's ability to ask the question of God, in the last analysis is a self-deception, as the use of human language in speaking of revelation shows.

The problem of the interdependence of existential questions and theological answers can be solved only within what, in the introductory part, was called the "theological circle." The theologian as theologian is committed to a concrete expression of the ultimate concern, religiously speaking, of a special revelatory experience. On the basis of this concrete experience, he makes his universal claims, as Christianity did in terms of the statement that Jesus as the Christ is the Logos. This circle can be understood as an ellipse (not as a geometrical circle) and described in terms of two central points—the existential question and the theological answer. Both are within the sphere of the religious commitment, but they are not identical. The material of the existential question is taken from the whole of human experience and its manifold ways of expression. This refers to past and present, to popular language and great literature, to art and philosophy, to science and psychology. It refers to myth and liturgy, to religious traditions, and to present experiences. All this, as far as it reflects man's existential predicament, is the material without the help of which the existential question cannot be formulated. The choice of the material, as well as the formulation of the question, is the task of the systematic theologian.

In order to do so, he must participate in the human predicament, not only actually—as he always does—but also in conscious identification. He must participate in man's finitude, which is also his own, and in its anxiety as though he had never received the revelatory answer of "eternity." He must participate in man's estrangement, which is also his own, and show the anxiety of guilt as though he had never received the revelatory answer of "forgiveness." The theologian does not rest on the theological answer which he announces. He can give it in a convincing way only if he participates with his whole being in the situation of the question, namely, the human predicament. In the light of this demand, the method of correlation protects the theologian from the arrogant claim of having revelatory answers at his disposal. In formulating the answer, he must struggle for it.

While the material of the existential question is the very expression of the human predicament, the form of the question is determined by the total system and by the answers given in it. The question implied in human finitude is directed toward the answer: the eternal. The question implied in human estrangement is directed toward the answer: forgiveness. This directedness of the questions does not take away their seriousness, but it gives them a form determined by the theological system as a whole. This is the sphere within which the correlation of existential questions and theological answers takes place.

The other side of the correlation is the influence of the existential questions on the theological answers. But it should be reaffirmed that the answers cannot be derived from the questions, that the substance of the answers—the revelatory experience—is independent of the questions. But the form of the theological answer is *not* independent of the form of the existential question. If theology gives the answer, "the

Christ," to the question implied in human estrangement, it does so differently, depending on whether the reference is to the existential conflicts of Jewish legalism, to the existential despair of Greek skepticism, or to the threat of nihilism as expressed in twentieth-century literature, art, and psychology. Nevertheless, the question does not create the answer. The answer, "the Christ," cannot be created by man, but man can receive it and express it according to the way he has asked for it.

The method of correlation is not safe from distortion; no theological method is. The answer can prejudice the question to such a degree that the seriousness of the existential predicament is lost. Or the question can prejudice the answer to such a degree that the revelatory character of the answer is lost. No method is a guaranty against such failures. Theology, like all enterprises of the human mind, is ambiguous. But this is not an argument against theology or against the method of correlation. As method, it is as old as theology. We have therefore not invented a new method, but have rather tried to make explicit the implications of old ones, namely, that of apologetic theology.

PART III

EXISTENCE AND THE CHRIST

I

EXISTENCE AND THE QUEST FOR THE CHRIST

A. EXISTENCE AND EXISTENTIALISM

1. The Etymology of Existence

TODAY whoever uses terms like "existence," "existential," or "existentialism" is obliged to show the way in which he uses them and the reasons why. He must be aware of the many ambiguities with which these words are burdened, in part avoidable, in part unavoidable. Further, he must show to which past and present attitudes and works he applies these terms. Attempts to clarify their meaning are numerous and divergent. Therefore, none of these attempts can be taken as being finally successful. A theology which makes the correlation of existence and the Christ its central theme must justify its use of the word "existence" and indicate both its philological and its historical derivation.

One of the ways to determine the meaning of an abused word is the etymological one, namely, to go back to its root meaning and try to gain a new understanding out of its roots. This has been done in all periods of the history of thought but is exaggerated by some scholars to such a degree that a reaction has started against the whole procedure. The nominalists of our day, like the old nominalists, consider words as conventional signs which mean nothing beyond the way in which they are used in a special group at a special time. The consequence of this attitude is that some words are invariably lost and must be replaced by others. But the nominalistic presupposition—that words are *only* conventional signs—must be rejected. Words are the results of the encounter of the human mind with reality. Therefore, they are not only signs but also symbols and cannot be replaced, as in the case of conventional signs, by other words. Hence they can be salvaged. Without this possibility, new languages would continuously have had to be invented in the fields of religion and the humanities. One of the important tasks of

19

theology is to regain the genuine power of classical terms by looking at the original encounter of mind and reality which created them.

The root meaning of "to exist," in Latin, *existere,* is to "stand out." Immediately one asks: "To stand out of what?" On the one hand, in English, we have the word "outstanding," which means standing out of the average level of things or men, being more than others in power and value. On the other hand, "standing out" in the sense of *existere* means that existence is a common characteristic of all things, of those which are outstanding and of those which are average. The general answer to the question of what we stand out of is that we stand out of non-being. "Things do exist" means they have being, they stand out of nothingness. But we have learned from the Greek philosophers (what they have learned from the lucidity and sensitivity of the Greek language) that non-being can be understood in two ways, namely, as *ouk on,* that is, absolute non-being, or as *me on,* that is, relative non-being. Existing, "to stand out," refers to both meanings of non-being. If we say that something exists, we assert that it can be found, directly or indirectly, within the corpus of reality. It stands out of the emptiness of absolute non-being. But the metaphor "to stand out" logically implies something like "to stand in." Only that which in some respect stands in can stand out. He who is outstanding rises above the average in which he stood and partly still stands. If we say that everything that exists stands out of absolute non-being, we say that it is in both being and non-being. It does not stand completely out of non-being. As we have said in the chapter on finitude (in the first volume), it is a finite, a mixture of being and non-being. To exist, then, would mean to stand out of one's own non-being.

But this is not sufficient because it does not take into consideration this question: How can something stand out of its own non-being? To this the answer is that everything participates in being, whether or not it exists. It participates in potential being before it can come into actual being. As potential being, it is in the state of relative non-being, it is not-yet-being. But it is not nothing. Potentiality is the state of real possibility, that is, it is more than a logical possibility. Potentiality is the power of being which, metaphorically speaking, has not yet realized its power. The power of being is still latent; it has not yet become manifest. Therefore, if we say that something exists, we say that it has left the state of mere potentiality and has become actual. It stands out of mere potentiality, out of relative non-being.

In order to become actual, it must overcome relative non-being, the state of *me on*. But, again, it cannot be completely out of it. It must stand out and stand in at the same time. An actual thing stands out of mere potentiality; but it also remains in it. It never pours its power of being completely into its state of existence. It never fully exhausts its potentialities. It remains not only in absolute non-being, as its finitude shows, but also in relative non-being, as the changing character of its existence shows. The Greeks symbolized this as the resistance of *me on,* of relative non-being, against the actualization of that which is potential in a thing.

Summarizing our etymological inquiry, we can say: Existing can mean standing out of absolute non-being, while remaining in it; it can mean finitude, the unity of being and non-being. And existing can mean standing out of relative non-being, while remaining in it; it can mean actuality, the unity of actual being and the resistance against it. But whether we use the one or the other meaning of non-being, existence means standing out of non-being.

2. The Rise of the Existentialist Problem

Etymological inquiries indicate directions, but they do not solve problems. The pointer given in the second answer to the question "Standing out of what?" is that of a split in reality between potentiality and actuality. This is the first step toward the rise of existentialism. Within the whole of being as it is encountered, there are structures which have no existence and things which have existence on the basis of structures. Treehood does not exist, although it has being, namely, potential being. But the tree in my back yard does exist. It stands out of the mere potentiality of treehood. But it stands out and exists only because it participates in that power of being which is treehood, that power which makes every tree a tree and nothing else.

This split in the whole of reality, expressed in the term "existence," is one of the earliest discoveries of human thought. Long before Plato, the prephilosophical and the philosophical mind experienced two levels of reality. We can call them the "essential" and the "existential" levels. The Orphics, the Pythagoreans, Anaximander, Heraclitus, and Parmenides were driven to their philosophy by the awareness that the

world they encountered lacked ultimate reality. But only in Plato does
the contrast between the existential and the essential being become an
ontological and ethical problem. Existence for Plato is the realm of mere
opinion, error, and evil. It lacks true reality. True being is essential
being and is present in the realm of eternal ideas, i.e., in essences. In
order to reach essential being, man must rise above existence. He must
return to the essential realm from which he fell into existence. In this
way man's existence, his standing out of potentiality, is judged as a fall
from what he essentially is. The potential is the essential, and to exist,
i.e., to stand out of potentiality, is the loss of true essentiality. It is not
a complete loss, for man still stands in his potential or essential being.
He remembers it, and, through his remembrance, he participates in
the true and the good. He stands in and out of the essential realm. In
this sense "standing out" has a meaning precisely opposite that of the
usual English usage. It means falling away from what man essentially
is.

This attitude toward existence dominated the later ancient world in
spite of the attempt of Aristotle to close the gap between essence and
existence through his doctrine of the dynamic interdependence of form
and matter in everything. But Aristotle's protest could not succeed,
partly because of the sociological conditions of later antiquity and partly
because Aristotle himself in his *Metaphysics* contrasts the whole of
reality with the eternal life of God, i.e., his self-intuition. Participation in the life of God requires the rise of the mind into the *actus purus*
of the divine being, which is above everything which is mixed with
non-being.

The scholastic philosophers, including both the Platonizing Franciscans and the Aristotelian Dominicans, accepted the contrast between
essence and existence for the world, but not for God. In God there is
no difference between essential and existential being. This implies that
the split is ultimately not valid and that it has no relevance for the
ground of being itself. God is eternally what he is. This was expressed
in the Aristotelian phrase that God is *actus purus,* without potentiality.
The logical consequence of this concept would have been the denial
of a living God such as is mirrored in biblical religion. But this was
not the intention of the Scholastics. The emphasis of Augustine and
Scotus on the divine will made that impossible. But if God is symbolized as will, the term *actus purus* is obviously inadequate. Will implies

potentiality. The real meaning of the Scholastic doctrine—which I consider to be true—would have been expressed in the statement that essence and existence and their unity must be applied symbolically to
God. He is not subjected to a conflict between essence and existing.
He is not a being beside others, for then his essential nature would
transcend himself, just as in the case of all finite beings. Nor is he the
essence of all essences, the universal essence, for this would deprive him
of the power of self-actualization. His existence, his standing out of
his essence, is an expression of his essence. Essentially, he actualizes
himself. He is beyond the split. But the universe is subject to the split.
God alone is "perfect," a word which is exactly defined as being beyond the gap between essential and existential being. Man and his
world do not have this perfection. Their existence stands out of their
essence as in a "fall." On this point, the Platonic and the Christian
evaluations of existence coincide.

This attitude changed when a new feeling for existence grew up in
the Renaissance and Enlightenment. More and more the gap between
essence and existence was closed. Existence became the place in which
man was called to control and to transform the universe. Existing
things were his material. To stand out of one's essential being was not
a fall but the way to the actualization and fulfilment of one's potentialities. In its philosophical form this attitude could be called "essentialism." In this sense existence is, so to speak, swallowed by essence.
The existing things and events are the actualization of essential being
in a progressive development. There are preliminary shortcomings, but
there is no existential gap as expressed in the myth of the Fall. In existence, man is what he is in essence—the microcosmos in whom the
powers of the universe are united, the bearer of critical and constructive reason, the builder of his world, and the maker of himself as the
actualization of his potentiality. Education and political organization
will overcome the lags of existence behind essence.

This description fits the spirit of many philosophers of the Renaissance and of the entire Enlightenment. But in neither period did essentialism come to fulfilment. This happened only in a philosophy
which was distinctly anti-enlightened and deeply influenced by Roman-
ticism, namely, German classical philosophy and, in particular, the
system of Hegel. The reason for this is not only the all-embracing
and consistent character of Hegel's system but also that he was aware of

the existentialist problem and tried to take existential elements into his universal system of essences. He took non-being into the very center of his thought; he stressed the role of passion and interest in the movement of history; he created concepts like "estrangement" and "unhappy consciousness"; he made freedom the aim of the universal process of existence; he even brought the Christian paradox into the frame of his system. But he kept all these existential elements from undermining the essentialist structure of his thought. Non-being has been conquered in the totality of the system; history has come to its end; freedom has become actual; and the paradox of the Christ has lost its paradoxical character. Existence is the logically necessary actuality of essence. There is no gap, no leap, between them. This all-embracing character of Hegel's system made it a turning point in the long struggle between essentialism and existentialism. He is the classical essentialist, because he applied to the universe the scholastic doctrine that God is beyond essence and existence. The gap is overcome not only eternally in God but also historically in man. The world is the process of the divine self-realization. There is no gap, no ultimate incertitude, no risk, and no danger of self-loss when essence actualizes itself in existence. Hegel's famous statement that everything that is, is reasonable is not an absurd optimism about the reasonableness of man. Hegel did not believe that men are reasonable and happy. But it is the statement of Hegel's belief that, in spite of everything unreasonable, the rational or essential structure of being is providentially actualized in the process of the universe. The world is the self-realization of the divine mind; existence is the expression of essence and not the fall away from it.

3. Existentialism against Essentialism

It was in protest to Hegel's perfect essentialism that the existentialism of the nineteenth and twentieth centuries arose. It was not a special trait of his thought which was criticized by the existentialists, some of whom were his pupils. They were not interested in correcting him. They attacked the essentialist idea as such, and with it the whole modern development of man's attitude toward himself and his world. Their attack was and is a revolt against the self-interpretation of man in modern industrial society.

The immediate attack on Hegel came from several sides. In systematic theology we cannot deal with the individual rebels, such as Schelling, Schopenhauer, Kierkegaard, or Marx. Suffice it to state that in these decades (1830–50) was prepared the historical destiny and the cultural self-expression of the Western world in the twentieth century. In systematic theology we must show the character of the existentialist revolt and confront the meaning of existence which has developed in it with the religious symbols pointing to the human predicament.

The common point in all existentialist attacks is that man's existential situation is a state of estrangement from his essential nature. Hegel is aware of this estrangement, but he believes that it has been overcome and that man has been reconciled with his true being. According to all the existentialists, this belief is Hegel's basic error. Reconciliation is a matter of anticipation and expectation, but not of reality. The world is not reconciled, either in the individual—as Kierkegaard shows—or in society—as Marx shows—or in life as such—as Schopenhauer and Nietzsche show. Existence is estrangement and not reconciliation; it is dehumanization and not the expression of essential humanity. It is the process in which man becomes a thing and ceases to be a person. History is not the divine self-manifestation but a series of unreconciled conflicts, threatening man with self-destruction. The existence of the individual is filled with anxiety and threatened by meaninglessness. With this description of man's predicament all existentialists agree and are therefore opposed to Hegel's essentialism. They feel that it is an attempt to hide the truth about man's actual state.

The distinction has been made between atheistic and theistic existentialism. Certainly there are existentialists who could be called "atheistic," at least according to their intention; and there are others who can be called "theistic." But, in reality, there is no atheistic or theistic existentialism. Existentialism gives an analysis of what it means to exist. It shows the contrast between an essentialist description and an existentialist analysis. It develops the question implied in existence, but it does not try to give the answer, either in atheistic or in theistic terms. Whenever existentialists give answers, they do so in terms of religious or quasi-religious traditions which are not derived from their existentialist analysis. Pascal derives his answers from the Augustinian tradition, Kierkegaard from the Lutheran, Marcel from the Thomist, Dostoevski from the Greek Orthodox. Or the answers are derived from humanistic traditions, as with Marx, Sartre, Nietzsche, Heidegger, and Jaspers. None of these men was able to develop answers out of his questions. The answers of the humanists come from hidden religious sources. They are matters of ultimate concern or faith, although garbed in a secular gown. Hence the distinction between atheistic and theistic existentialism fails. Existentialism is an analysis of the human predicament. And the answers to the questions implied in man's predicament are religious, whether open or hidden.

questionable

4. EXISTENTIAL AND EXISTENTIALIST THINKING

For the sake of further philological clarification, it is useful to distinguish between existential and existentialist. The former refers to a human attitude, the latter to a philosophical school. The opposite of existential is detached; the opposite of existentialist is essentialist. In existential thinking, the object is involved. In non-existential thinking, the object is detached. By its very nature, theology is existential; by its very nature, science is non-existential. Philosophy unites elements of both. In intention, it is non-existential; in reality, it is an ever changing combination of elements of involvement and detachment. This makes futile all attempts to create a so-called "scientific philosophy."

Existential is not existentialist, but they are related in having a common root, namely, "existence." Generally speaking, one can describe essential structures in terms of detachment, and existential predicament in terms of involvement. But this statement needs drastic qualifications. There is an element of involvement in the construction of geometrical figures; and there is an element of detachment in the observation of one's own anxiety and estrangement. The logician and mathematician are driven by *eros,* including desire and passion. The existentialist theologian, who analyzes existence, discovers structures through cognitive detachment, even if they are structures of destruction. And between these poles there are many mixtures of detachment and involvement, as in biology, history, and psychology. Nevertheless, a cognitive attitude in which the element of involvement is dominant is called "existential." The converse is also true. Since the element of involvement is so dominant, the most striking existentialist analyses have been made by novelists, poets, and painters. But even they could escape irrelevant subjectivity only by submitting themselves to detached and objective observation. As a result, the material brought out by the detached methods of therapeutic psychology are used in existentialist literature and art. Involvement and detachment are poles, not conflicting alternatives; there is no existentialist analysis without non-existential detachment.

5. Existentialism and Christian Theology

Christianity asserts that Jesus is the Christ. The term "the Christ" points by marked contrast to man's existential situation. For the Christ, the Messiah, is he who is supposed to bring the "new eon," the universal regeneration, the new reality. New reality presupposes an old reality; and this old reality, according to prophetic and apocalyptic descriptions, is the state of the estrangement of man and his world from God. This estranged world is ruled by structures of evil, symbolized as demonic powers. They rule individual souls, nations, and even nature. They produce anxiety in all its forms. It is the task of the Messiah to conquer them and to establish a new reality from which the demonic powers or the structures of destruction are excluded.

Existentialism has analyzed the "old eon," namely, the predicament of man and his world in the state of estrangement. In doing so, existentialism is a natural ally of Christianity. Immanuel Kant once said that mathematics is the good luck of human reason. In the same way, one could say that existentialism is the good luck of Christian theology. It has helped to rediscover the classical Christian interpretation of human existence. Any theological attempt to do this would not have had the same effect. This positive use refers not only to existentialist philosophy but also to analytic psychology, literature, poetry, drama, and art. In all these realms there is an immense amount of material which the theologian can use and organize in the attempt to present Christ as the answer to the questions implied within existence. In earlier centuries a similar task was undertaken mainly by monastic theologians, who analyzed themselves and the members of their small community so penetratingly that there are few present-day insights into the human predicament which they did not anticipate. The penitential and devotional literature impressively shows this. But this tradition was lost under the impact of the philosophies and theologies of pure consciousness, represented, above all, by Cartesianism and Calvinism. Notwithstanding differences, they were allies in helping to repress the unconscious and half-conscious sides of human nature, thus preventing a full understanding of man's existential predicament (in spite of Calvin's doctrine of man's total depravity and the Augustinianism of the Cartesian school). In recovering the elements of man's nature which were suppressed by the psychology of consciousness, existentialism and contemporary theology should become allies and analyze the character of existence in all its manifestations, the unconscious as well as the conscious.

The systematic theologian cannot do this alone; he needs the help of creative representatives of existentialism in all realms of culture. He needs the support of the practical explorers of man's predicament, such as ministers, educators, psychoanalysts, and counselors. The theologian must reinterpret the traditional religious symbols and theological concepts in the light of the material he receives from these people. He must be aware of the fact that terms like "sin" and "judgment" have lost not their truth but rather an expressive power which can be regained only if they are filled with the insights into human nature which existentialism (including depth psychology) has given to us. Now the biblicistic theologian is right in maintaining that all these insights can be found in the Bible. And the Roman Catholic is equally right in pointing to these insights in the Church Fathers. The question is not whether something can be found somewhere—almost everything can— but whether a period is ripe for rediscovering a lost truth. For example, he who reads Ecclesiastes or Job with eyes opened by existentialist analyses will see more in either than he was able to see before. The same is true of many other passages of the Old and New Testaments.

Existentialism has been criticized as being too "pessimistic." Terms like "non-being," "finitude," "anxiety," "guilt," "meaninglessness," and "despair" seem to justify such criticism. Criticism also has been directed against much biblical writing, as, for instance, Paul's description of the human predicament in Romans, chapters 1 and 7. But Paul is pessimistic (in the sense of hopeless) in these passages only if they are read in isolation and without the answer to the question implied in them.

Certainly this is not the case within a theological system. The word "pessimism" should be avoided in connection with descriptions of human nature, for it is a mood, not a concept or description. From the point of view of systematic structure, it must be added that the existential elements are only one part of the human predicament. They are always combined ambiguously with essential elements; otherwise they would have no being at all. Essential as well as existential elements are always abstractions from the concrete actuality of being, namely, "Life." This is the subject of the fourth part of *Systematic Theology*. For the sake of analysis, however, abstractions are necessary, even if they have a strongly negative sound. And no existentialist analysis of the human predicament can escape this, even if it is hard to bear—as the doctrine of sin always has been in traditional theology.

B. THE TRANSITION FROM ESSENCE TO EXISTENCE AND THE SYMBOL OF "THE FALL"

1. THE SYMBOL OF "THE FALL"AND WESTERN PHILOSOPHY

The symbol of "the Fall" is a decisive part of the Christian tradition. Although usually associated with the biblical story of the "Fall of Adam," its meaning transcends the myth of Adam's Fall and has universal anthropological significance. Biblical literalism did a distinct disservice to Christianity in its identification of the Christian emphasis on the symbol of the Fall with the literalistic interpretation of the Genèsis story. Theology need not take literalism seriously, but we must realize how its impact has hampered the apologetic task of the Christian church. Theology must clearly and unambiguously represent "the Fall" as a symbol for the human situation universally, not as the story of an event that happened "once upon a time."

In order to sharpen this understanding, the phrase "transition from essence to existence" is used in this system. It is, so to speak, a "half-way demythologization" of the myth of the Fall. The element of "once upon a time" is removed. But the demythologization is not complete, for the phrase "transition from essence to existence" still contains a temporal element. And if we speak in temporal terms about the divine, we still speak in mythical terms, even if such abstract concepts as "essence" and "existence" replace mythological states and figures. Complete demythologization is not possible when speaking about the divine. When Plato described the transition from essence to existence, he used a mythological form of expression—in speaking of the "Fall of the soul." He knew that existence is not a matter of essential necessity but that it is a fact and that therefore the "Fall of the soul" is a story to be told in mythical symbols. If he had understood existence to be a logical implication of essence, existence itself would have appeared as essential. Symbolically speaking, sin would be seen as created, as a necessary consequence of man's essential nature. But sin is not created, and the transition from essence to existence is a fact, a story to be told and not a derived dialectical step. Therefore, it cannot be completely demythologized.

At this point idealism as well as naturalism stand against the Christian (and Platonic) symbol of the Fall. Essentialism in Hegel's system was fulfilled in idealistic terms. In it, as in all idealism, the Fall is reduced to the difference between ideality and reality, and reality is then seen as pointing toward the ideal. The Fall is not a break, but an imperfect fulfilment. It approximates fulfilment in the historical process or is fulfilled in principle in the present period of history. Christianity and existentialism consider the progressivistic (or revolutionary) form of the idealistic faith as utopianism, and the conservative form as ideology. Both are interpreted as self-deception and idolatry. Neither takes the self-contradicting power of human freedom and the demonic implication of history seriously.

The Fall, in the sense of the transition from essence to existence, is denied not only by idealism but also by naturalism—from the other side, so to speak. The latter takes existence for granted, without asking about the source of its negativity. It does not try to answer the question of why man is aware of negativity as something that should not be and for which he is responsible. Symbols such as the Fall, descriptions of the human predicament, and concepts such as "estrangement" and "man against himself" are strongly, even cynically, rejected. "Man has no predicament," I heard a naturalistic philosopher say. Naturalists, however, usually avoid resignation or cynicism by including elements of idealism either in their progressivistic form or in the more realistic form of Stoicism. In both forms, pure naturalism is transcended, but the symbol of the Fall is not reached. This is not even achieved in ancient Stoicism's belief in the deterioration of man's historical existence and in the gap between the fools and the wise ones. Neo-Stoicism is impregnated with so many idealistic elements that it does not reach the full depth of Christian realism.

When a Christian symbol such as the Fall is confronted with philosophies like idealism, naturalism, or neo-Stoicism, one may well ask whether it is possible to relate ideas which lie on different levels, the one on the level of religious symbolism, the other on the level of philosophical concepts. But, as explained in the section on philosophy and theology in the first volume, there is an interpenetration of levels between theology and philosophy. If the idealist or naturalist asserts that "there is no human predicament," he makes an existential decision about a matter of ultimate concern. In expressing his decision in conceptual terms, he is a theologian. And if the theologian says that existence is estranged from essence, not only does he make an existential decision, but, in expressing it in ontological concepts, he is a philosopher. The philosopher cannot avoid existential decisions, and the theologian cannot avoid ontological concepts. Although their intentions are opposite, their actual procedures are comparable. This justifies our comparison of the symbol of the Fall with Western philosophical thought and the alliance of existentialism and theology.

2. Finite Freedom as the Possibility of the Transition from Essence to Existence

The story of Genesis, chapters 1–3, if taken as a myth, can guide our description of the transition from essential to existential being. It is the profoundest and richest expression of man's awareness of his existential estrangement and provides the scheme in which the transition from essence to existence can be treated. It points, first, to the possibility of the Fall; second, to its motives; third, to the event itself; and, fourth, to its consequences. This will be the order and scheme of the following sections.

In the part entitled "Being and God," the polarity of freedom and destiny was discussed in relation to being as such, as well as in relation to human beings. On the basis of the solution given there, we can answer the question of how the transition from essence to existence is possible in terms of "freedom," which is always in polar unity with destiny. But this is only a first step to the answer. In the same section of the first volume, we described man's awareness of his finitude and of finitude universally, and we analyzed the situation of being related to and excluded from infinity. This provides the second step toward an answer. It is not freedom as such, but finite freedom. Man has freedom in contrast to all other creatures. They have analogies to freedom but not freedom itself. But man is finite, excluded from the infinity to which he belongs. One can say that nature is finite necessity, God is infinite freedom, man is finite freedom. It is finite freedom which makes possible the transition from essence to existence.

Man is free, in so far as he has language. With his language, he has universals which liberate him from bondage to the concrete situation to which even the highest animals are subjected. Man is free, in so far as he is able to ask questions about the world he encounters, including himself, and to penetrate into deeper and deeper levels of reality. Man is free, in so far as he can receive unconditional moral and logical imperatives which indicate that he can transcend the conditions which determine every finite being. Man is free, in so far as he has the power of deliberating and deciding, thus cutting through the mechanisms of stimulus and response. Man is free, in so far as he can play and build imaginary structures above the real structures to which he, like all beings, is bound. Man is free, in so far as he has the faculty of creating worlds above the given world, of creating the world of technical tools and products, the world of artistic expressions, the world of theoretical structures and practical organizations. Finally, man is free, in so far as he has the power of contradicting himself and his essential nature. Man is free even from his freedom; that is, he can surrender his humanity. This final quality of his freedom provides the third step toward the answer to the question of how the transition from essence to existence is possible.

Man's freedom is finite freedom. All the potentialities which constitute his freedom are limited by the opposite pole, his destiny. In nature, destiny has the character of necessity. In spite of analogies to human destiny, God is his own destiny. This means that he transcends the polarity of freedom and destiny. In man freedom and destiny limit each other, for he has finite freedom. This is true of every act of human freedom; it is true also of the final quality of human freedom, namely, the power of surrendering his freedom. Even the freedom of self-contradiction is limited by destiny. As finite freedom, it is possible only within the context of the universal transition from essence to existence. There is no individual Fall. In the Genesis story the two sexes and nature, represented by the serpent, work together. The transition from essence to existence is possible because finite freedom works within the frame of a universal destiny; this is the fourth step toward the answer.

Traditional theology discussed the possibility of the Fall in terms of Adam's *potuit peccare*—his freedom to sin. This freedom was not seen in unity with the total structure of his freedom and therefore was considered as a questionable divine gift. Calvin thought the freedom to fall to be a weakness of man, regrettable from the point of view of man's happiness, since it meant eternal condemnation for most human beings (e.g., all pagans). This gift is understandable only from the point of view of the divine glory, in that God decided to reveal his majesty not only through salvation but also through the condemnation of men. But the freedom of turning away from God is a quality of the structure of freedom as such. The possibility of the Fall is dependent on all the qualities of human freedom taken in their unity. Symbolically speaking, it is the image of God in man which gives the possibility of the Fall. Only he who is the image of God has the power of separating himself from God. His greatness and his weakness are identical. Even God could not remove the one without removing the other. And if man had not received this possibility, he would have been a thing among things, unable to serve the divine glory, either in salvation or in condemnation. Therefore, the doctrine of the Fall has always been treated as the doctrine of the Fall of man, although it was also seen as a cosmic event.

3. "Dreaming Innocence" and Temptation

Having discussed how the transition from essence to existence is possible, we now come to the question of the motifs driving to the transition. In order to answer this, we must have an image of the state of essential being in which the motifs are working. The difficulty is that the state of essential being is not an actual stage of human development which can be known directly or indirectly. The essential nature of man is present in all stages of his development, although in existential distortion. In myth and dogma man's essential nature has been projected into the past as a history before history, symbolized as a golden age or paradise. In psychological terms one can interpret this state as that of "dreaming innocence." Both words point to something that precedes actual existence. It has potentiality, not actuality. It has no place, it is *ou topos* (utopia). It has no time; it precedes temporality, and it is suprahistorical. Dreaming is a state of mind which is real and non-real at the same time—just as is potentiality. Dreaming anticipates the actual, just as everything actual is somehow present in the potential. In the moment of awakening, the images of the dream disappear as images and return as encountered realities. Certainly, reality is different from the images of the dream, but not totally different. For the actual is present in the potential in terms of anticipation. For these reasons the metaphor "dreaming" is adequate in describing the state of essential being.

The word "innocence" also points to non-actualized potentiality. One is innocent only with respect to something which, if actualized, would end the state of innocence. The word has three connotations. It can mean lack of actual experience, lack of personal responsibility, and lack of moral guilt. In the metaphorical use suggested here, it is meant in all three senses. It designates the state before actuality, existence, and history. If the metaphor "dreaming innocence" is used, concrete connotations appear, taken from human experience. One is reminded of the early stages of a child's development. The most striking example is the growth of his sexual consciousness. Up to a certain point, the child is unconscious of his sexual potentialities. In the difficult steps of transition from potentiality to actuality, an awakening takes place. Experience, responsibility, and guilt are acquired, and the state of dreaming innocence is lost. This example is evident in the biblical story, where sexual consciousness is the first consequence of the loss of innocence. One should not confuse this metaphorical use of the term "innocence" with the false assertion that the newborn human being is in a state of sinlessness. Every life always stands under the conditions of existence. The word "innocence," like the word "dreaming," is used not in its proper but in its analogical sense. But, if used in this way, it can provide a psychological approach to the state of essential or potential being.

The state of dreaming innocence drives beyond itself. The possibility of the transition to existence is experienced as temptation. Temptation is unavoidable because the state of dreaming innocence is uncontested and undecided. It is not perfection. Orthodox theologians have heaped perfection after perfection upon Adam before the Fall, making him equal with the picture of the Christ. This procedure is not only absurd; it makes the Fall completely unintelligible. Mere potentiality or dreaming innocence is not perfection. Only the conscious union of existence and essence is perfection, as God is perfect because he transcends essence and existence. The symbol "Adam before the Fall" must be understood as the dreaming innocence of undecided potentialities.

If we ask what it is that drives dreaming innocence beyond itself, we must continue our analysis of the concept "finite freedom." Man is not only finite, as is every creature; he is also aware of his finitude. And this awareness is "anxiety." In the last decade the term "anxiety" has become associated with the German and Danish word *Angst,* which itself is derived from the Latin *angustiae,* "narrows." Through Søren Kierkegaard the word *Angst* has become a central concept of existentialism. It expresses the awareness of being finite, of being a mixture of being and non-being, or of being threatened by non-being. All creatures are driven by anxiety; for finitude and anxiety are the same. But in man freedom is united with anxiety. One could call man's freedom "freedom in anxiety" or "anxious freedom" (in German, *sich ängstigende Freiheit*). This anxiety is one of the driving forces toward the transition from essence to existence. Kierkegaard particularly has used the concept of anxiety to describe (not to explain) the transition from essence to existence.

Using this idea and analyzing the structure of finite freedom, one may show in two interrelated ways the motifs of the transition from essence to existence. There is an element in the Genesis story which has often been overlooked—the divine prohibition not to eat from the tree of knowledge. Any command presupposes that what is commanded is not yet fulfilled. The divine prohibition presupposes a kind of split between creator and creature, a split which makes a command necessary, even if it is given only in order to test the obedience of the creature. This cleavage is the most important point in the interpretation of the Fall. For it presupposes a sin which is not yet sin but which is also no longer innocence. It is the desire to sin. I suggest calling the state of this desire "aroused freedom." In the state of dreaming innocence, freedom and destiny are in harmony, but neither of them is actualized. Their unity is essential or potential; it is finite and therefore open to tension and disruption—just like uncontested innocence. The tension occurs in the moment in which finite freedom becomes conscious of itself and tends to become actual. This is what could be called the moment of aroused freedom. But in the same moment a reaction starts, coming from the essential unity of freedom and destiny. Dreaming innocence wants to preserve itself. This reaction is symbolized in the biblical story as the divine prohibition against actualizing one's potential freedom and against acquiring knowledge and power. Man is caught between the desire to actualize his freedom and the demand to preserve his dreaming innocence. In the power of his finite freedom, he decides for actualization.

The same analysis can be made, so to speak, from the inside, namely, from man's anxious awareness of his finite freedom. At the moment when man becomes conscious of his freedom, the awareness of his dangerous situation gets hold of him. He experiences a double threat, which is rooted in his finite freedom and expressed in anxiety. Man experiences the anxiety of losing himself by not actualizing himself and his potentialities and the anxiety of losing himself by actualizing himself and his potentialities. He stands between the preservation of his dreaming innocence without experiencing the actuality of being and the loss of his innocence through knowledge, power, and guilt. The anxiety of this situation is the state of temptation. Man decides for self-actualization, thus producing the end of dreaming innocence.

Again it is sexual innocence which psychologically gives the most adequate analogy to the preceding. The typical adolescent is driven by the anxiety of losing himself, either in the actualization of himself sexually or in his non-actualization sexually. On the one hand, the taboos imposed on him by society have power over him in confirming his own anxiety about losing his innocence and becoming guilty by actualizing his potentiality. On the other hand, he is afraid of not actualizing himself sexually and of sacrificing his potentialities by preserving his innocence. He usually decides for actualization, as men universally do. Exceptions (e.g., for the sake of conscious asceticism) limit the analogy to the human situation generally, but they do not remove the analogy.

The analysis of temptation, as given here, makes no reference to a conflict between the bodily and the spiritual side of man as a possible cause. The doctrine of man indicated here implies a "monistic" understanding of man's nature in contrast to a dualistic one. Man is a whole man, whose essential being has the character of dreaming innocence, whose finite freedom makes possible the transition from essence to existence, whose aroused freedom puts him between two anxieties which threaten the loss of self, whose decision is against the preservation of dreaming innocence and for self-actualization. Mythologically speaking, the fruit of the tree of temptation is both sensuous and spiritual.

4. The Moral and the Tragic Element in the Transition from Essential to Existential Being

The transition from essence to existence is the original fact. It is not the first fact in a temporal sense or a fact beside or before others, but it is that which gives validity to every fact. It is the actual in every fact. We do exist and our world with us. This is the original fact. It means that the transition from essence to existence is a universal quality of finite being. It is not an event of the past; for it ontologically precedes everything that happens in time and space. It sets the conditions of spatial and temporal existence. It is manifest in every individual person in the transition from dreaming innocence to actualization and guilt.

If the transition from essence to existence is expressed mythologically —as it must be in the language of religion—it is seen as an event of the past, although it happens in all three modes of time. The event of the past to which traditional theology refers is the story of the Fall as told in the Book of Genesis. Perhaps no text in literature has received so many interpretations as the third chapter of Genesis. This is partly due to its uniqueness—even in biblical literature—partly to its psychological profundity, and partly to its religious power. In mythological language it describes the transition from essence to existence as a unique event which happened long ago in a special place to individual persons—first to Eve, then to Adam. God himself appears as an individual person in time and space as a typical "father figure." The whole description has a psychological-ethical character and is derived from the daily experiences of people under special cultural and social conditions. Nevertheless, it has a claim to universal validity. The predominance of psychological and ethical aspects does not exclude other factors in the biblical story. The serpent represents the dynamic trends of nature; there is the magical character of the two trees, the rise of sexual consciousness, the curse over the heredity of Adam, the body of the woman, the animals and the land.

These traits show that a cosmic myth is hidden behind the psychological-ethical form of the story and that the prophetic "demythologization" of this myth has not removed, but rather subordinated, the mythical elements to the ethical point of view. The cosmic myth reappears in the Bible in the form of the struggle of the divine with demonic powers and the powers of chaos and darkness. It reappears also in the myth of the Fall of the angels and in the interpretation of the serpent of Eden as the embodiment of a fallen angel. These examples all point to the cosmic presuppositions and implications of the Fall of Adam. But the most consistent emphasis on the cosmic character of the Fall is given in the myth of the transcendent Fall of the souls. While it probably has Orphic roots, it is first told by Plato when he contests essence and existence. It received a Christian form by Origen, a humanistic one by Kant, and is present in many other philosophies and theologies of the Christian Era. All have recognized that existence cannot be derived from within existence, that it cannot be derived from an individual event in time and space. They have recognized that existence has a universal dimension.

The myth of the transcendent Fall is not directly biblical, but neither does it contradict the Bible. It affirms the ethical-psychological element in the Fall and carries through the cosmic dimensions which we find in biblical literature. The motif of the myth of the transcendent Fall is the tragic-universal character of existence. The meaning of the myth is that the very constitution of existence implies the transition from essence to existence. The individual act of existential estrangement is not the isolated act of an isolated individual; it is an act of freedom which is imbedded, nevertheless, in the universal destiny of existence. In every individual act the estranged or fallen character of being actualizes itself. Every ethical decision is an act both of individual freedom and of universal destiny. This justifies both forms of the myth of the Fall. Obviously, both are myths and are absurd if taken literally instead of symbolically. Existence is rooted both in ethical freedom and in tragic destiny. If the one or the other side is denied, the human situation becomes incomprehensible. Their unity is the great problem of the doctrine of man. Of all the aspects of the cosmic myth of Genesis, the doctrine of "original sin" has been most violently attacked since the early eighteenth century. This concept was the first point criticized by the Enlightenment, and its rejection is one of the last points defended by contemporary humanism. Two reasons explain the violence with which the modern mind has fought against the idea of original sin. First, its mythological form was taken literally by attackers and defenders and therefore was unacceptable to an awakening, historical-critical way of thinking. Second, the doctrine of original sin seemed to imply a negative evaluation of man, and this radically contradicted the new feeling for life and world as it had developed in industrial society. It was feared that the pessimism about man would inhibit the tremendous impulse of modern man, technically, politically, and educationally to transform world and society. There was and still is the apprehension that authoritarian and totalitarian consequences could follow from a negative valuation of man's moral and intellectual power. Theology must join— and in most cases has done so—the historical-critical attitude toward the biblical and ecclesiastical myth. Theology further must emphasize the positive valuation of man in his essential nature. It must join classical humanism in protecting man's created goodness against naturalistic and existentialistic denials of his greatness and dignity. At the same time, theology should reinterpret the doctrine of original sin by

showing man's existential self-estrangement and by using the helpful
existentialist analyses of the human predicament. In doing so, it must
develop a realistic doctrine of man, in which the ethical and the tragic
element in his self-estrangement are balanced. It may well be that such
a task demands the definite removal from the theological vocabulary
of terms like "original sin" or "hereditary sin" and their replacement
by a description of the interpenetration of the moral and the tragic elements in the human situation.

The empirical basis for such a description has become quite extensive in our period. Analytic psychology, as well as analytic sociology,
has shown how destiny and freedom, tragedy and responsibility, are
interwoven in every human being from early childhood on and in all
social and political groups in the history of mankind. The Christian
church has maintained a stable balance of both sides in its description
of the human situation, although frequently in inadequate language
and always in conflicting directions. Augustine fought for a way between Manichaeism and Pelagianism; Luther rejected Erasmus but
was interpreted by Flacius Illyricus in a half-Manichaean way; the
Jansenists were accused by the Jesuits of destroying man's rationality;
liberal theology is criticized by neo-orthodoxy as well as by a kind of
existentialism (e.g., Sartre, Kafka) which has some Manichaean traits.
Christianity cannot escape these tensions. It must simultaneously acknowledge the tragic universality of estrangement and man's personal
responsibility for it.

5. CREATION AND FALL

The unity of the moral and the tragic element in man's predicament
leads to the question of the relationship of man with the universe in existence and consequently to the question of creation and the Fall. In non-
biblical as well as biblical myths man is held responsible for the Fall,
though it is conceived as a cosmic event, as the universal transition from
essential goodness to existential estrangement. In the myths subhuman
and superhuman figures influence the decision of man. But man himself
makes the decision and receives the divine curse for it. In the Genesis
story it is the serpent which represents the dynamics of nature in and
around man. But, alone, the serpent is without power. Only through
man can transition from essence to existence occur. Later doctrines
combined the symbol of rebellious angels with the symbol of the ser-

pent. But even this was not supposed to release man from his responsibility; for the Fall of Lucifer, though resulting in man's temptation, does not cause his Fall. The myth of the Fall of the angels does not help to solve the riddle of existence. It introduces an even darker riddle, namely, how "blessed spirits," who eternally perceive the divine glory, could be tempted to turn away from God. This way of interpreting the Fall of man needs more explanation than the Fall itself. The myth can be criticized because it confuses powers of being with beings. The truth of the doctrine of angelic and demonic powers is that there are supra-individual structures of goodness and supra-individual structures of evil. Angels and demons are mythological names for constructive and destructive powers of being, which are ambiguously interwoven and which fight with each other in the same person, in the same social group, and in the same historical situation. They are not beings but powers of being dependent on the whole structure of existence and involved in the ambiguous life. Man is responsible for the transition from essence to existence because he has finite freedom and because all dimensions of reality are united in him.

On the other hand, we have seen that man's freedom is imbedded in universal destiny and that therefore the transition from essence to existence has both moral and tragic character. This makes it necessary to ask how universal existence is related to man's existence. In respect to the Fall, how is man related to nature? And if the universe participates in the Fall in the same way, what is the relation between creation and the Fall?

Biblical literalism would answer that the Fall of man changed the structures of nature. The divine curse upon Adam and Eve involves a change of nature in and around man. If such literalism is rejected as absurd, then what does the term "fallen world" mean? If the structures of nature were always what they are now, can one speak of the participation of nature, including man's natural basis, in his existential estrangement? Has nature been corrupted by man? Does this combination of words have any meaning at all?

The first answer to these questions is that the transition from essence to existence is not an event in time and space but the transhistorical quality of all events in time and space. This is equally true of man and of nature. "Adam before the Fall" and "nature before the curse" are states of potentiality. They are not actual states. The actual state is that existence in which man finds himself along with the whole universe, and there is no time in which this was otherwise. The notion of a moment *in* time in which man and nature were changed from good to evil is absurd, and it has no foundation in experience or revelation.

In view of this statement, one may ask whether it is not less confusing to drop the concept of the fallen world and to distinguish radically between man and nature. Is it not more realistic to state that man alone is able to become guilty because he is able to make responsible decisions and that nature is innocent? Such a division is accepted by many people because it seems to solve a rather difficult problem in a simple way. But it is too simple to be true. It leaves out the tragic element, the element of destiny, in man's predicament. If estrangement were based only on the responsible decisions of the individual person, each individual could always either contradict or not contradict his essential nature. There would be no reason to deny that people could avoid and have avoided sin altogether. This was the Pelagian view, even if Pelagius had to admit that bad examples influence the decisions of free and responsible individuals. There is no such thing as "bondage of the will" in this view. The tragic element of man's predicament, manifest from earliest infancy, is disregarded. In the Christian tradition men like Augustine, Luther, and Calvin have rejected this view. Pelagian ideas were rejected by the early church, and semi-Pelagian ideas, which have become strong in the medieval church, were rejected by the Reformers. The neo-Pelagian ideas of contemporary moralistic Protestantism are rejected by neo-orthodox and existentialist theologians. Christianity knows and can never give up its knowledge of the tragic universality of existential estrangement.

This means, however, that Christianity must reject the idealistic separation of an innocent nature from guilty man. Such a rejection has become comparatively easy in our period because of the insights gained about the growth of man and his relation to nature within and outside himself. First, it can be shown that in the development of man there is no absolute discontinuity between animal bondage and human freedom. There are leaps between different stages, but there is also a slow and continuous transformation. It is impossible to say at which point in the process of natural evolution animal nature is replaced by the nature which, in our present experience, we know as human, a nature which is qualitatively different from animal nature. The possibility that both natures were in conflict with each other in the same being cannot be denied. Second, one cannot decide at which points in the development of the human individual responsibility begins and ends. Legal thought attributes it rather late to the individual. And even in the mature man there are limits to responsibility. Some of them are so drastic as to be acknowledged in morals and law. "Responsibility" presupposes the fully developed ability to "respond" as a person. But there are many stages of reduced centeredness caused by tiredness, sickness, intoxication, neurotic compulsions, and psychotic splits. All this does not remove responsibility, but it shows the element of destiny in every act of freedom. Third, we must refer to the present rediscovery of the unconscious and its determining power in man's conscious decisions. The way in which this happens has been described in past and present existentialist literature as well as in the psychoanalytic movements of our period. One of the most striking facts about the dynamics of the human personality is the intentional ignorance concerning one's real motives. The motives themselves are bodily and psychic strivings, often far removed from what appears as conscious reason in a centered decision. Such a decision is still free, but it is freedom within the limits of destiny. Fourth, the social dimension of unconscious strivings must be considered. The questionable term "collective unconscious" points to the reality of this dimension. The centered self is dependent not only on the influences of its social surroundings which are consciously given and received but also on those which are effective in a society without being apprehended and formulated. All this shows that the independence within an individual decision is only half the truth.

Biological, psychological, and sociological powers are effective in every individual decision. The universe works through us as part of the universe.

At this point someone may say that, while such considerations refute Pelagian moral freedom, they establish a Manichaean tragic destiny! But that is not the case. Moral freedom becomes "Pelagian" only if it is separated from tragic destiny; and tragic destiny becomes "Manichaean" only if it is separated from moral freedom. They belong to each other. Freedom is not the freedom of indeterminacy. That would make every moral decision an accident, unrelated to the person who acts. But freedom is the possibility of a total and centered act of the

personality, an act in which all the drives and influences which constitute the destiny of man are brought into the centered unity of a decision. None of these drives compels the decision in isolation. (Only in
states of disintegration is the personality determined by compulsions.)
But they are effective in union and through the deciding center. In this
way the universe participates in every act of human freedom. It represents the side of destiny in the act of freedom.

Conversely, there are analogies to freedom effective in all parts of
the universe. From the atomic structures to the most highly developed
animals, there are total and centered reactions which can be called
"spontaneous" in the dimension of organic life. Of course, structured
and spontaneous reactions in the non-human nature are not responsible actions and do not constitute guilt. But it does not seem adequate,
either, to apply the adjective "innocent" to nature. Logically, it is not
correct to speak of innocence where there is no possibility of becoming
guilty. And, as there are analogies to human freedom in nature, so
there are also analogies to human good and human evil in all parts of
the universe. It is worthy of note that Isaiah prophesied peace in nature for the new eon, thereby showing that he would not call nature
"innocent." Nor would the writer who, in Genesis, chapter 3, tells
about the curse over the land declare nature innocent. Nor would Paul
do so in Romans, chapter 8, when he speaks about the bondage to fu-
tility which is the fate of nature. Certainly, all these expressions are
poetic-mythical. They could not be otherwise, since only poetic empathy
opens the inner life of nature. Nevertheless, they are realistic in substance and certainly more realistic than the moral utopianism which
confronts immoral man with innocent nature. Just as, within man, nature participates in the good and evil he does, so nature, outside man,
shows analogies to man's good and evil doing. Man reaches into nature,
as nature reaches into man. They participate in each other and cannot
be separated from each other. This makes it possible and necessary to
use the term "fallen world" and to apply the concept of existence (in
contrast to essence) to the universe as well as to man.

The tragic universality of existence, the element of destiny in human
freedom, and the symbol of the "fallen world" naturally raise the question as to whether sin is made ontologically necessary instead of a matter of personal responsibility and guilt. Does not the preceding description "ontologize away" the reality of the Fall and estrangement? These

questions become rather urgent if one states (and it must be stated) that there is a point in which creation and the Fall coincide, in spite of their logical difference.

The answer to these questions (which have been asked by several critics of the first volume, notably Reinhold Niebuhr in his contribution to the book *The Theology of Paul Tillich*) is an interpretation of the statement about the coincidence of creation and the Fall. Creation and the Fall coincide in so far as there is no point in time and space in which created goodness was actualized and had existence. This is a necessary consequence of the rejection of the literal interpretation of the paradise story. There was no "utopia" in the past, just as there will be no "utopia" in the future. Actualized creation and estranged existence are identical. Only biblical literalism has the theological right to deny this assertion. He who excludes the idea of a historical stage of essential goodness should not try to escape the consequence. This is even more obvious if one applies the symbol of creation to the whole temporal process. If God creates here and now, everything he has created participates in the transition from essence to existence. He creates the newborn child; but, if created, it falls into the state of existential estrangement. This is the point of coincidence of creation and the Fall. But it is not a logical coincidence; for the child, upon growing into maturity, affirms the state of estrangement in acts of freedom which imply responsibility and guilt. Creation is good in its essential character. If actualized, it falls into universal estrangement through freedom and destiny. The hesitation of many critics to accept these obviously realistic statements is caused by their justified fear that sin may become a rational necessity, as in purely essentialist systems. Against them theology must insist that the leap from essence to existence is the original fact—that it has the character of a leap and not of structural necessity. In spite of its tragic universality, existence cannot be derived from essence.

C. THE MARKS OF MAN'S ESTRANGEMENT AND THE CONCEPT OF SIN

1. ESTRANGEMENT AND SIN

The state of existence is the state of estrangement. Man is estranged from the ground of his being, from other beings, and from himself. The transition from essence to existence results in personal guilt and universal tragedy. It is now necessary to give a description of existential estrangement and its self-destructive implications. But, before doing so, we must answer the question which has already arisen: What is the relation of the concept of estrangement to the traditional concept of sin?

"Estrangement" as a philosophical term was created and applied by Hegel, especially in his doctrine of nature as estranged mind (*Geist*). But his discovery of estrangement happened long before he developed his philosophy of nature. In his early fragments he described life-processes as possessing an original unity which is disrupted by the split into subjectivity and objectivity and by the replacement of love by law. It is this concept of estrangement, rather than the one in his philosophy of nature, which was used against Hegel by some of his pupils, especially Marx. They rejected Hegel's contention that estrangement is overcome by reconciliation in history. The individual is estranged and not reconciled; society is estranged and not reconciled; existence is estrangement. In the strength of this insight, they become revolutionaries against the world as it existed and were existentialists long before the beginning of the twentieth century.

In the sense in which it was used by the anti-Hegelians, estrangement points to the basic characteristic of man's predicament. Man as he exists is not what he essentially is and ought to be. He is estranged from his true being. The profundity of the term "estrangement" lies in the implication that one belongs essentially to that from which one is estranged. Man is not a stranger to his true being, for he belongs to it. He is judged by it but cannot be completely separated, even if he is hostile to it. Man's hostility to God proves indisputably that he belongs to him. Where there is the possibility of hate, there and there alone is the possibility of love.

Estrangement is not a biblical term but is implied in most of the biblical descriptions of man's predicament. It is implied in the symbols of the expulsion from paradise, in the hostility between man and nature, in the deadly hostility of brother against brother, in the estrangement of nation from nation through the confusion of language, and in the continuous complaints of the prophets against their kings and people who turn to alien gods. Estrangement is implied in Paul's statement that man perverted the image of God into that of idols, in his classical description of "man against himself," in his vision of man's hostility against man as combined with his distorted desires. In all these interpretations of man's predicament, estrangement is implicitly asserted. Therefore, it is certainly not unbiblical to use the term "estrangement" in describing man's existential situation.

Nevertheless, "estrangement" cannot replace "sin." Yet the reasons for attempts to replace the word "sin" with another word are obvious. The term has been used in a way which has little to do with its genuine biblical meaning. Paul often spoke of "Sin" in the singular and without an article. He saw it as a quasi-personal power which ruled this world. But in the Christian churches, both Catholic and Protestant, sin has been used predominantly in the plural, and "sins" are deviations from moral laws. This has little to do with "sin" as the state of estrangement from that to which one belongs—God, one's self, one's world. Therefore, the characteristics of sin are here considered under the heading of "estrangement." And the word "estrangement" itself implies a reinterpretation of sin from a religious point of view.

Nevertheless, the word "sin" cannot be overlooked. It expresses what is not implied in the term "estrangement," namely, the personal act of turning away from that to which one belongs. Sin expresses most sharply the personal character of estrangement over against its tragic side. It expresses personal freedom and guilt in contrast to tragic guilt and the universal destiny of estrangement. The word "sin" can and must be saved, not only because classical literature and liturgy continuously employ it but more particularly because the word has a sharpness which accusingly points to the element of personal responsibility in one's estrangement. Man's predicament is estrangement, but his estrangement is sin. It is not a state of things, like the laws of nature, but a matter of both personal freedom and universal destiny. For this reason the term "sin" must be used after it has been reinterpreted religiously. An important tool for this reinterpretation is the term "estrangement."

Reinterpretation is also needed for the terms "original" or "hereditary" with respect to sin. But in this case reinterpretation may demand the rejection of the terms. Both point to the universal character of estrangement, expressing the element of destiny in estrangement. But both words are so much burdened with literalistic absurdities that it is practically impossible to use them any longer.

If one speaks of "sins" and refers to special acts which are considered as sinful, one should always be conscious of the fact that "sins" are the expressions of "sin." It is not the disobedience to a law which makes an act sinful but the fact that it is an expression of man's estrangement from God, from men, from himself. Therefore, Paul calls everything sin which does not result from faith, from the unity with God. And in another context (following Jesus) all laws are summed up in the law of love by which estrangement is conquered. Love as the striving for the reunion of the separated is the opposite of estrangement. In faith and love, sin is conquered because estrangement is overcome by reunion.

2. ESTRANGEMENT AS "UNBELIEF"

The Augsburg Confession defines sin as the state of man in which he is "without faith in God and with concupiscence" (*sine fide erga deum et cum concupiscentia*). One could add to these two expressions of estrangement a third one, namely *hubris* (ὕβρις), the so-called spiritual sin of pride or self-elevation, which, according to Augustine and Luther, precedes the so-called sensual sin. This gives the three concepts of "unbelief," "concupiscence," and *hubris* as the marks of man's estrangement. Each of them needs reinterpretation in order to mediate insights into man's existential predicament.

Unbelief, in the view of the Reformers, is not the unwillingness or inability to believe the doctrines of the church, but, like faith, it is an act of the total personality, including practical, theoretical, and emotional elements. If there were such a word as "un-faith," it should be used instead of the word "unbelief." The latter has an unavoidable connotation associated with the term "belief," which came to mean the acceptance of statements without evidence. "Unbelief" for Protestant Christianity means the act or state in which man in the totality of his being turns away from God. In his existential self-realization he turns toward himself and his world and loses his essential unity with the ground of his being and his world. This happens both through individual responsibility and through tragic universality. It is freedom and destiny in one and the same act. Man, in actualizing himself, turns to himself and away from God in knowledge, will, and emotion. Unbelief is the disruption of man's cognitive participation in God. It should not be called the "denial" of God. Questions and answers, whether positive or negative, already presuppose the loss of a cognitive union with God. He who asks for God is already estranged from God, though not cut off from him. Unbelief is the separation of man's will from the will of God. It should not be called "disobedience"; for command, obedience, and disobedience already presuppose the separation of will from will. He who needs a law which tells him how to act or how not to act is already estranged from the source of the law which demands obedience. Unbelief is also the empirical shift from the blessedness of the divine life to the pleasures of a separated life. It should not be called "self-love." In order to have a self which not only can be loved but can love God, one's center must already have left the divine center to which it belongs and in which self-love and love to God are united.

All this is implied in the term "unbelief." It is the first mark of estrangement, and its character justifies the term "estrangement." Man's unbelief is his estrangement from God in the center of his being. This is the religious understanding of sin as rediscovered by the Reformers and as lost again in most Protestant life and thought.

If unbelief is understood as man's estrangement from God in the center of his self, then the Augustinian interpretation of sin as love turned away from God to self can be accepted by Protestant theology. Un-faith is ultimately identical with un-love; both point to man's estrangement from God. For Augustine, sin is the love which desires finite goods for their own sake and not for the sake of the ultimate good. Love of one's self and one's world can be justified if it affirms everything finite as a manifestation of the infinite and wants to be united with it for this reason. Love of one's self and one's world is distorted if it does not penetrate through the finite to its infinite ground. If it turns away from the infinite ground to its finite manifestations, then it is unbelief. The disruption of the essential unity with God is the innermost character of sin. It is estrangement in terms of faith as well as in terms of love.

There is, however, a difference between the two definitions of sin. In the concept of faith an element of "in spite of" is implied, the courage to accept that one is accepted in spite of sin, estrangement, and despair. If this question is asked—and asked as passionately and desperately as the Reformers did—the primacy of faith is established. This reunion of the estranged with God is "reconciliation." It has the character of "in spite of," since it is God who wants us to be reconciled with him. For this reason Protestantism holds to the primacy of faith, both in the doctrine of sin and in the doctrine of salvation.

For Augustine the union between God and man is re-established by the mystical power of grace through the mediation of the church and its sacraments. Grace, as the infusion of love, is the power which overcomes estrangement. Therefore, for Augustine and the Roman Catholic church, love has primacy in the doctrine of sin as well as in the doctrine of salvation. For the Reformers, estrangement is overcome by personal reconciliation with God and by the love which follows this reconciliation. For Augustine, estrangement is overcome by the infused love of God and the faith which is doctrinally expressed by the Roman Catholic church. But in spite of this profound difference, there is a point at which the two doctrines converge. Both emphasize the religious character of sin, as indicated in the term "estrangement." The first mark of estrangement—unbelief—includes un-love. Sin is a matter of our relation to God and not to ecclesiastical, moral, or social authorities. Sin is a religious concept, not in the sense that it is used in religious contexts, but in the sense that it points to man's relation to God in terms of estrangement and possible reunion.

3. Estrangement as "Hubris"

In estrangement, man is outside the divine center to which his own center essentially belongs. He is the center of himself and of his world. The possibility of leaving his essential center—and, with this possibility, the temptation—is given because structurally he is the only fully centered being. He alone has not only consciousness (which is a high, but incomplete, centeredness) but self-consciousness or complete centeredness. This structural centeredness gives man his greatness, dignity, and being, the "image of God." It indicates his ability to transcend both himself and his world, to look at both, and to see himself in perspective as the center in which all parts of his world converge. To be a self and to have a world constitute the challenge to man as the perfection of creation.

But this perfection is, at the same time, his temptation. Man is tempted to make himself existentially the center of himself and his world. When looking at himself and his world, he realizes his freedom and, with it, his potential infinity. He realizes that he is not bound to any special situation or element in it. But, at the same time, he knows that he is finite. It was this situation which induced the Greeks to call men "the mortals" and to attribute man's potential infinity to the gods, calling them "the immortals." Man could create the images of the immortal gods only because he was aware of his own potential infinity. Standing between actual finitude and potential infinity enables him to call men and only men "mortals" (although all beings have to die) and to call the divine images of men the "immortals." If man does not acknowledge this situation—the fact that he is excluded from the infinity of the gods—he falls into *hubris*. He elevates himself beyond the limits of his finite being and provokes the divine wrath which destroys him. This is the main subject of Greek tragedy.

The word *hubris* cannot be adequately translated, although the reality to which it points is described not only in Greek tragedy but also in the Old Testament. It is most distinctly expressed in the serpent's promise to Eve that eating from the tree of knowledge will make man equal to God. *Hubris* is the self-elevation of man into the sphere of the divine. Man is capable of such self-elevation because of his greatness. In Greek tragedy, human *hubris* is represented not by the small, ugly, and average but by heroes who are great, beautiful, and outstanding, who are the bearers of power and value. In the same way the prophets of the Old Testament threaten the great in the nation—the kings, the priests, the judges, the wealthy, and the beautiful. And they threaten the whole nation, that nation which they consider to be the greatest of all, the elected one, Israel. By its intrinsic dynamics, greatness drives toward *hubris*. Only a few men represent greatness in the tragedy of human history. But every human being participates in greatness and is represented by the few. The greatness of man lies in his being infinite, and it is just this temptation of *hubris* into which he universally falls through destiny and freedom. Therefore, one should not translate *hubris* as "pride." Pride is a moral quality, whose opposite is humility. *Hubris* is not the special quality of man's moral character. It is universally human; it can appear in acts of humility as well as in acts of pride. Although it is possible to enlarge the meaning of pride to include *hubris*, it seems to be less confusing to use the term "self-elevation" for *hubris*.

Hubris has been called the "spiritual sin," and all other forms of sin have been derived from it, even the sensual ones. *Hubris* is not one form of sin beside others. It is sin in its total form, namely, the other side of unbelief or man's turning away from the divine center to which he belongs. It is turning toward one's self as the center of one's self and one's world. This turning toward one's self is not an act done by a

special part of man, such as his spirit. Man's whole life, including his
sensual life, is spiritual. And it is in the totality of his personal being
that man makes himself the center of his world. This is his *hubris;*
this is what has been called "spiritual sin." Its main symptom is that
man does not acknowledge his finitude. He identifies partial truth with
ultimate truth, as, e.g., Hegel did when he claimed to have created a
final system containing the whole of possible truth. The existentialist
and naturalist reactions against his system and the catastrophe in con
sequence of these attacks were the answer to his metaphysical *hubris,*
his ignoring of man's finitude. In a similar way, people have identified
their limited goodness with absolute goodness, as, for example, the
Pharisees and their successors in Christianity and in secularism. Here
also tragic self-destruction followed *hubris,* as the catastrophes of Juda- / anti-Semitic
ism, Puritanism, and bourgeois moralism have shown. And man identi-
fies his cultural creativity with divine creativity. He attributes infinite
significance to his finite cultural creations, making idols of them, elevat-
ing them into matters of ultimate concern. The divine answer to man's
cultural *hubris* comes in the disintegration and decay of every great
culture in the course of history.

These examples are taken from forms of *hubris* which have historical
significance and transcend individual destiny. They show irrefutably
the universally human character of self-elevation. But the self-elevation
of a group happens through the self-elevation of individuals. Every individual within and outside the group falls into moments of *hubris.*
All men have the hidden desire to be like God, and they act accord-
ingly in their self-evaluation and self-affirmation. No one is willing to
acknowledge, in concrete terms, his finitude, his weakness and his
errors, his ignorance and his insecurity, his loneliness and his anxiety.
And if he is ready to acknowledge them, he makes another instrument
of *hubris* out of his readiness. A demonic structure drives man to confuse natural self-affirmation with destructive self-elevation.

4. Estrangement as "Concupiscence"

The quality of all acts in which man affirms himself existentially has
two sides, the one in which he removes his center from the divine center (unbelief) and the other in which he makes himself the center of
himself and of his world (*hubris*). The question naturally arises concerning why man is tempted to become centered in himself. The an-

swer is that it places him in the position of drawing the whole of his world into himself. It elevates him beyond his particularity and makes him universal on the basis of his particularity. This is the temptation of man in his position between finitude and infinity. Every individual, since he is separated from the whole, desires reunion with the whole. His "poverty" makes him seek for abundance. This is the root of love in all its forms. The possibility of reaching unlimited abundance is the temptation of man who is a self and has a world. The classical name for this desire is *concupiscentia* "concupiscence"—the unlimited desire to draw the whole of reality into one's self. It refers to all aspects of man's relation to himself and to his world. It refers to physical hunger as well as to sex, to knowledge as well as to power, to material wealth as well as to spiritual values. But this all-embracing meaning of "concupiscence" has often been reduced to a rather special meaning, namely, the striving for sexual pleasure. Even theologians like Augustine and Luther, who considered the spiritual sin as basic, had the tendency to identify concupiscence with sexual desire. This is understandable in Augustine, who never overcame the Hellenistic and especially the Neo-Platonic devaluation of sex. But it is inconsistent and difficult to understand that remnants of this tradition appear in the theology and the ethics of the Reformers. They do not always clearly reject the un-Protestant doctrine that "hereditary" sin is rooted in sexual pleasure in the act of propagation. If "concupiscence" is used in this limited sense, it is certainly unable to describe the state of general estrangement, and it would be better to drop it completely. For the ambiguity of the word "concupiscence" is one of many expressions giving rise to the ambiguity of the Christian attitude toward sex. The church has never been able to deal adequately with this central ethical and religious problem. A restatement of the meaning of "concupiscence" may be a valuable help in overcoming this situation.

The doctrine of concupiscence—taken in its all-embracing sense—can be supported by much material and deeper insights from existentialist literature, art, philosophy, and psychology. It will suffice to mention first a few examples, some of them expressing the meaning of concupiscence in symbolic figures, others expressing it in analyses. When Kierkegaard describes the figure of the Emperor Nero, he takes up an early Christian motif and uses it for a psychology of concupiscence. Nero embodies the demonic implications of unlimited power; he represents the particular individual who has succeeded in drawing the universe into himself in terms of the power to use for himself whatever he wants to use. Kierkegaard describes the complete inner emptiness of this situation, which leads to the determination to bring death to everything he encounters, including himself. In a similar way he interprets the figure of Mozart's Don Juan, creating the additional figure of Johannes, the seducer. Here, with the same psychological penetration, he shows the emptiness and despair of that unlimited sexual striving which prevents a creative union of love with the sexual partner. Here, as in the symbol of Nero, the self-defying character of concupiscence is visible. One could add a third example, the figure of Goethe's Faust, whose unlimited striving is directed toward knowledge which subordinates both power and sex. In order to "know everything," he accepts the pact with the devil. It is the "everything," not knowledge as such, which produces the demonic temptation. Knowledge as such, just as power and sex as such, is not a matter of concupiscence, but it is the desire cognitively to draw the universe into one's self and one's finite particularity.

It is the unlimited character of the strivings for knowledge, sex, and power which makes them symptoms of concupiscence. This is elaborated in two conceptual descriptions of concupiscence, Freud's "libido" and Nietzsche's "will to power." Both these concepts have contributed immensely to a rediscovery of the Christian view of man's predicament. But both ignore the contrast between man's essential and his existential being and interpret man exclusively in terms of existential concupiscence, omitting any reference to man's essential *eros* which is related to a definite content.

Libido in Freud is the unlimited desire of man to get rid of his biological, especially his sexual, tensions and to get pleasure from the discharge of these tensions. Freud has shown that libidinous elements are present in the highest spiritual experiences and activities of man, and, in doing so, he has rediscovered insights which can be found in the monastic traditions of self-scrutiny as they had been developed in early and medieval Christianity. Freud's emphasis on these elements, which cannot be separated from man's sexual instincts, is justified and agrees with the realism of the Christian interpretation of man's predicament. It should not be rejected in the name of dishonest pseudo-Christian taboos against sex. Freud in his honest realism is more Christian than are these taboos. He describes, from a special angle, exactly what concupiscence means. This is especially obvious in the way Freud describes the consequences of concupiscence and its never satisfied striving. When he speaks of the "death instinct" (*Todestrieb,* better translated by the "drive for death"), he describes the desire to escape the pain of the never satisfied libido. Like every higher being, man desires to return to the lower level of life out of which he has arisen. The pain inflicted by the higher level drives toward the lower. It is the never satisfied libido in man, whether repressed or unrestrained, which produces in him the desire to get rid of himself as man. In these observations concerning man's "discontent" with his creativity, Freud looks deeper into the human predicament than many of his followers and critics. Up to this point, a theological interpreter of man's estrangement is well advised to follow Freud's analyses.

But theology cannot accept Freud's doctrine of libido as a sufficient reinterpretation of the concept of concupiscence. Freud did not see that his description of human nature is adequate for man only in his existential predicament but not in his essential nature. The endlessness of libido is a mark of man's estrangement. It contradicts his essential or created goodness. In man's essential relation to himself and to his world, libido is not concupiscence. It is not the infinite desire to draw the universe into one's particular existence, but it is an element of love united with the other qualities of love—*eros, philia,* and *agape.* Love does not exclude desire; it receives libido into itself. But the libido which is united with love is not infinite. It is directed, as all love is, toward a definite subject with whom it wants to unite the bearer of love. Love wants the other being, whether in the form of libido, *eros, philia,* or *agape.* Concupiscence, or distorted libido, wants one's own pleasure through the other being, but it does not want the other being. This is the contrast between libido as love and libido as concupiscence. Freud did not make this distinction because of his puritanical attitude toward sex. Only through repression and sublimation of libido can man become creative. In Freud's thought there is no creative *eros* which includes sex. In comparison with a man like Luther, Freud is ascetic in his basic assumption about the nature of man. Classical Protestantism denies these assumptions in so far as man in his essential or created nature is concerned; for in man's essential nature the desire to be united with the object of one's love for its own sake is effective. And this desire is not infinite but definite. It is not concupiscence but love.

The analysis of Freud's concept of libido has produced important insights into the nature of concupiscence and its opposite. Another concept, equally important for Christian theology, is Nietzsche's "will to power." One of the ways in which it has influenced recent thought is through those depth psychologists who have interpreted human libido more in terms of power than in terms of sex. But there are other, more direct, ways in which Nietzsche's concept has influenced contemporary thought, especially in politics and in social theory. "Will to power" is partly a concept, partly a symbol. Therefore, it must not be understood literally. "Will to power" means neither will as a conscious psychological act nor power as the control of men by men. The conscious will to gain power over men is rooted in the unconscious desire to affirm one's own power of being. "Will to power" is an ontological symbol for man's natural self-affirmation in so far as man has the power of being. But it is not restricted to man, it is a quality of everything that is. It belongs to created goodness of the will to power and is a strong symbol of the dynamic self-realization which characterizes life.

But, like Freud's "libido," Nietzsche's "will to power" is also blurred if described in such a way that the distinction between man's essential self-affirmation and his existential striving for power of being without limit is not clearly established. Nietzsche follows Schopenhauer's doctrine of the will as the unlimited driving power in all life, producing in man the desire to come to rest through the self-negation of the will. In this respect the analogy between Schopenhauer and Freud is obvious. In both cases it is the infinite, never satisfied drive which leads to self-negation. Nietzsche tries to overcome this trend by emphatically proclaiming a courage which takes the negativities of being into itself. In this he is influenced by Stoicism and Protestantism. But, in contrast to both of them, he does not show the norms and principles by which the will to power can be judged. It remains unlimited and has demonic-destructive traits. It is another concept and symbol of concupiscence.

Neither libido in itself nor the will to power in itself is a characteristic of concupiscence. Both become expressions of concupiscence and estrangement when they are not united with love and therefore have no definite object.

5. Estrangement as Fact and as Act

Classical theology has distinguished between original and actual sin. "Original sin" is Adam's act of disobedience and the sinful disposition produced by his act in every human being. Therefore, original sin has also been called hereditary sin (*Erbsünde* in German). Adam's fall, in this view, has corrupted the whole human race. The way in which this happened was described differently; but the result, i.e., that mankind as a whole lives in estrangement, was generally accepted. Therefore, no one can escape sin; estrangement has the character of universal human destiny. However, the combination of man's predicament with a completely free act by Adam is inconsistent as well as literally absurd. It exempts a human individual from the universal human character by ascribing freedom to him without destiny (just as destiny without freedom was asserted of the Christ in some types of Christology). But the former dehumanizes Adam, as the latter dehumanizes the Christ. Adam must be understood as essential man and as symbolizing the transition from essence to existence. Original or hereditary sin is neither original nor hereditary; it is the universal destiny of estrangement which concerns every man. When Augustine spoke of a *massa perditionis,* a "mass of perdition," he expressed the insight, in opposition to Pelagius, that man in his estrangement is a social being and cannot be isolated into a subject able to make free decisions. The unity of destiny and freedom must be preserved in the description of every condition of man.

Sin is a universal fact before it becomes an individual act, or more precisely, sin as an individual act actualizes the universal fact of estrangement. As an individual act, sin is a matter of freedom, responsibility, and personal guilt. But this freedom is imbedded in the universal destiny of estrangement in such a way that in every free act the destiny of estrangement is involved and, vice versa, that the destiny of estrangement is actualized by all free acts. Therefore, it is impossible to separate sin as fact from sin as act. They are interwoven, and their unity is an immediate experience of everyone who feels himself to be guilty. Even if one takes the full responsibility for an act of estrangement—as one should—one is aware that this act is dependent on one's whole being, including free acts of the past and the destiny which is one's special, as well as mankind's universal, destiny.

Estrangement as fact has been explained in deterministic terms: physically, by a mechanistic determinism; biologically, by theories of the decadence of the biological power of life; psychologically, as the compulsory force of the unconscious; sociologically, as the result of class domination; culturally, as the lack of educational adjustment. None of these explanations accounts for the feeling of personal responsibility that man has for his acts in the state of estrangement. But each of these theories contributes to an understanding of the element of destiny in the human predicament. In this sense Christian theology must accept each of them; but it must add that no description of the element of destiny in the state of estrangement can remove the experience of finite freedom and, consequently, the responsibility for every act in which estrangement is actualized. Deterministic explanations of man's predicament do not necessarily deny his personal responsibility, as the determinist himself practically acknowledges in a situation in which, for instance, coercion is applied to make him recant his deterministic conviction. In this situation he feels his responsibility, whether he resists or submits. And it is this experience that matters in describing the human predicament, not a hypothetical explanation of the causes of his decision. The doctrine of the universality of estrangement does not make man's consciousness of guilt unreal; but it does liberate him from the unrealistic assumption that in every moment he has the undetermined freedom to decide in whatever way he chooses—for good or bad, for God or against him.

From the time of the biblical period the Christian church divided actual sins into mortal and venial sins, according to their seriousness. Later it added capital sins but always drew a sharp line between sins before and after baptism. These differences are decisive for the functioning of the priests in respect to the individual Christian's use of the sacraments and for his anticipation of eternal destiny; for the different kinds of sins are in strict correspondence to the different types of grace in this and the future life. The point of orientation for this conception and its practice is through the psychological and educational interest of the Roman Catholic church. The church looks at the extent of personal participation and guilt in a sinful act, and it is right in weighing the differences in guilt—just as the judge does if he weighs responsibility and punishment. But the whole scheme of quantities and relativities becomes irreligious the moment that it is applied to man's relation to God. Protestantism considered this issue in respect to both sin and grace. There is only "the Sin," the turning-away from God, and from "the Grace," or reunion with God. These are qualitative and absolute, not quantitative and relative, categories. Sin is estrangement; grace is reconciliation. Precisely because God's reconciling grace is unconditional, man does not need to look at his own condition and the degrees of his guilt. He has the certainty of total forgiveness in the situation of total guilt. This is the consoling power of the Protestant understanding of sin and grace concerning one's relation to God. It gives a certainty which the Catholic position can never acknowledge. At the same time, Protestantism must acknowledge that, under the impact of sin and grace as absolute categories, it has lost much of the psychological insight and the educational flexibility of the Catholic position. It has often deteriorated to a rigid moralism, which is just the opposite of the original Protestant intention. The breakdown of this moralism under the influence of depth psychology should be the first step toward a re-evaluation of the Catholic insights into the infinite complexities of man's spiritual life and toward the necessity of dealing with the relative, as well as the absolute, elements in sin and grace. The rise of "counseling" in the parish duties of the Protestant minister is an important step in this direction.

6. Estrangement Individually and Collectively

The description of estrangement given thus far deals exclusively with the individual person, his freedom and destiny, his guilt and possible reconciliation. In connection with recent events, as in the case of nations, the question of collective guilt has become urgent. It was never completely absent from human consciousness, for there were always ruling individuals, classes, and movements which committed acts against man's essential nature and brought destruction upon the group to which they belonged. Judaism and Christianity placed emphasis on the personal guilt of the individual, but they could not overlook issues such as the suffering of children due to the sins of the parents. Social condemnation of personally innocent descendants of morally condemned parents was not unknown in the Christian Era. And lately whole nations have been morally condemned for the atrocities of their rulers and of many individuals who were coerced into crime through their rulers. A confession of guilt was demanded of the whole nation, including those who resisted the ruling group and suffered because of their resistance.

The latter point shows that there is a fundamental difference between a person and a social group. In contrast to the centered individual whom we call a "person," the social group has no natural, deciding center. A social group is a power structure, and in every power structure certain individuals determine the actions of all individuals who are parts of the group. There is, therefore, always a potential or real conflict within the group, even if the outcome is the united action of the group as a whole. As such, a social group is not estranged, and, as such, a social group is not reconciled. There is no collective guilt. But there is the universal destiny of mankind, which, in a special group, becomes special destiny without ceasing to be universal. Every individual participates in this destiny and cannot extricate himself.

And destiny is inseparably united with freedom. Therefore, individual guilt participates in the creation of the universal destiny of mankind and in the creation of the special destiny of the social group to which a person belongs. The individual is not guilty of the crimes performed by members of his group if he himself did not commit them. The citizens of a city are not guilty of the crimes committed in their city; but they are guilty as participants in the destiny of man as a whole and in the destiny of their city in particular; for their acts in which freedom was united with destiny have contributed to the destiny in which they participate. They are guilty, not of committing the crimes of which their group is accused, but of contributing to the destiny in which these crimes happened. In this indirect sense, even the victims of tyranny in a nation are guilty of this tyranny. But so are the subjects of other nations and of mankind as a whole. For the destiny of falling under the power of a tyranny, even a criminal tyranny, is a part of the universal destiny of man to be estranged from what he essentially is.

If accepted, such considerations would restrain victorious nations from exploiting their victory in the name of the assumed "collective guilt" of the conquered nation. And they would constrain every individual within the conquered nation, even if he suffered in consequence of his resistance against the crimes committed by her, to accept part of the responsibility for the destiny of his nation. He himself, perhaps unwittingly and unwillingly but nevertheless responsibly, helped to prepare, or to retain, or to aggravate the conditions out of which the actual crime developed.

D. EXISTENTIAL SELF-DESTRUCTION AND
THE DOCTRINE OF EVIL

1. Self-Loss and World-Loss in the State of Estrangement

Man finds himself, together with his world, in existential estrangement, unbelief, *hubris,* and concupiscence. Each expression of the estranged state contradicts man's essential being, his potency for goodness. It contradicts the created structure of himself and his world and their interdependence. And self-contradiction drives toward self-destruction. The elements of essential being which move against each other tend to annihilate each other and the whole to which they belong. Destruction under the conditions of existential estrangement is not caused by some external force. It is not the work of special divine or demonic interferences, but it is the consequence of the structure of estrangement itself. One can describe this structure with a seemingly paradoxical term, "structure of destruction"—pointing to the fact that destruction has no independent standing in the whole of reality but that it is dependent on the structure of that in and upon which it acts destructively. Here, as everywhere in the whole of being, non-being is dependent on being, the negative on the positive, death on life. Therefore, even destruction has structures. It "aims" at chaos; but, as long as chaos is not attained, destruction must follow the structures of wholeness; and if chaos is attained, both structure and destruction have vanished.

As previously shown, the basic structure of finite being is the polarity of self and world. Only in man is this polarity fulfilled. Only man has a completely centered self and a structured universe to which he belongs and at which he is able to look at the same time. All other beings within our experience are only partly centered and consequently bound to their environment. Man also has environment, but he has it as a part of his world. He can and does transcend it with every word he speaks. He is free to make his world into an object which he beholds, and he is free to make himself into an object upon which he looks. In this situation of finite freedom he can lose himself and his world, and the loss of one necessarily includes the loss of the other. This is the basic "structure of destruction," and it includes all others. The analysis of this structure is the first step to the understanding of what is often described as "evil."

The term "evil" can be used in a larger and in a narrower sense. The larger sense covers everything negative and includes both destruction and estrangement—man's existential predicament in all its characteristics. If the word is used in this sense, sin is seen as one evil beside others. It is sometimes called "moral evil," namely, the negation of the morally good. One of the reasons for the use of "evil" in this larger sense is the fact that sin can appear in both functions, that is, as the cause of self-destruction and as an element of self-destruction—as when self-destruction signifies increased sin as the result of sin. In classical language, God punishes sin by throwing the sinner into more sin. Here sin is both the cause of evil and the evil itself. It should always be remembered that, even in this case, sin is evil because of its self-destructive consequences.

In the light of the preceding, it might be more appropriate to use the word in a narrower sense, namely, as the consequences of the state of sin and estrangement. In that case one can distinguish the doctrine of evil from the doctrine of sin. This is the sense in which the word will be used in the following sections. Hence the doctrine of evil follows the doctrine of sin, delineated in previous chapters. This procedure has the additional advantage of clarifying the concepts dealing with the problem of theodicy. If one is asked how a loving and almighty God can permit evil, one cannot answer in the terms of the question as it was asked. One must first insist on an answer to the question How could he permit sin?—a question which is answered the moment it is asked. Not permitting sin would mean not permitting freedom; this would deny the very nature of man, his finite freedom. Only after this answer can one describe evil as the structure of self-destruction which is implicit in the nature of universal estrangement.

theodicy

Self-loss as the first and basic mark of evil is the loss of one's determining center; it is the disintegration of the centered self by disruptive drives which cannot be brought into unity. So long as they are centered, these drives constitute the person as a whole. If they move against one another, they split the person. The further the disruption goes, the more the being of man as man is threatened. Man's centered self may break up, and, with the loss of self, man loses his world.

Self-loss is the loss of one's determining center, the disintegration of the unity of the person. This is manifest in moral conflicts and in psychopathological disruptions, independently or interdependently. The horrifying experience of "falling to pieces" gets hold of the person. To the degree in which this happens, one's world also falls to pieces. It ceases to be a world, in the sense of a meaningful whole. Things no longer speak to man; they lose their power to enter into a meaningful encounter with man, because man himself has lost this power. In extreme cases the complete unreality of one's world is felt; nothing is left except the awareness of one's own empty self. Such experiences are extreme, but extreme situations reveal possibilities in the ordinary situation. Possibilities of disruption are always present in man as a fully centered being. He cannot take his centeredness for granted. It is a form but not an empty one. It is actual only in unity with its content. The form of centeredness gives to the self the center which it needs to be what it is. There is no empty self, no pure subjectivity. Under the control of *hubris* and concupiscence, the self can approach the state of disintegration. The attempt of the finite self to be the center of everything gradually has the effect of its ceasing to be the center of anything. Both self and world are threatened. Man becomes a limited self, in dependence on a limited environment. He has lost his world; he has only his environment.

This fact includes the basic criticism of the environmental theories of man. They assert a view of man's essential nature which actually describes man's existential estrangement *from* his essential nature. Man essentially has a world because he has a fully centered self. He is able to transcend every given environment in the direction of his world. Only the loss of his world subjects him to the bondage of an environment which is not really *his* environment, namely, the result of a creative encounter with his world represented by a part of it. Man's true environment is the universe, and every special environment is qualified as a section of the universe. Only in estrangement can man be described as a mere object of environmental impact.

2. The Conflicts in the Ontological Polarities
    in the State of Estrangement

a) *The separation of freedom from destiny.*—The interdependence of self-loss and world-loss in the state of estrangement is manifest in the interdependent loss of the polar elements of being. The first of these are freedom and destiny. In essential being, i.e., the state of dreaming innocence, freedom and destiny lie within each other, distinct but not separated, in tension but not in conflict. They are rooted in the ground of being, i.e., the source of both of them and the ground of their polar unity. In the moment of aroused freedom a process starts in which freedom separates itself from the destiny to which it belongs. It becomes arbitrariness. Wilful acts are acts in which freedom moves toward the separation from destiny. Under the control of *hubris* and concupiscence, freedom ceases to relate itself to the objects provided by destiny. It relates itself to an indefinite number of contents. When man makes himself the center of the universe, freedom loses its definiteness. Indefinitely and arbitrarily, freedom turns to objects, persons, and things which are completely contingent upon the choosing subject and which therefore can be replaced by others of equal contingency and ultimate unrelatedness. Existentialism, supported by depth psychology, described the dialectics of this situation in terms of the restlessness, emptiness, and meaninglessness connected with it. If no essential relation between a free agent and his objects exists, no choice is objectively preferable to any other; no commitment to a cause or a person is meaningful; no dominant purpose can be established. The indications coming from one's destiny remain unnoticed or are disregarded. This certainly is the description of an extreme situation; but in its radicalism it can reveal a basic trend in the state of universal estrangement.

To the degree to which freedom is distorted into arbitrariness, destiny is distorted into mechanical necessity. If man's freedom is not directed by destiny or if it is a series of contingent acts of arbitrariness, it falls under the control of forces which move against one another without a deciding center. What seems to be free proves to be conditioned by internal compulsions and external causes. Parts of the self overtake the center and determine it without being united with the other parts. A contingent motive replaces the center which is supposed to unite the motives in a centered decision; but it is unable to do so. This is the ontological character of the state described in classical theology as the "bondage of the will." In view of this "structure of destruction," one could say: Man has used his freedom to waste his freedom; and it is his destiny to lose his destiny.

The distortion of freedom into arbitrariness and of destiny into mechanical necessity is mirrored in the traditional controversy between indeterminism and determinism. Like the environmental theory of man, indeterminism as well as determinism is a theory of man's essential nature in terms which are descriptions of man's estranged nature. Indeterminism makes man's freedom a matter of contingency. In doing so, it removes the very responsibility which it tried to preserve against determinism. And determinism surrenders man's freedom to mechanical necessity, transforming him into a completely conditioned thing which, as such, has no destiny—not even the destiny of having a *true* theory of determinism; for under the control of mechanical necessity there is neither truth nor destiny. Indeterminism, as well as determinism, is a mirror of man's state of estrangement (with respect to freedom and destiny!).

b) *The separation of dynamics from form.*—Every living being (and, in terms of analogy, every being) drives beyond itself and beyond the given form through which it has being. In man's essential nature, dynamics and form are united. Even if a given form is transcended, this happens in terms of form. In essential being there are forms of the self-transcendence of form. Their unity with the dynamics of being is never disrupted. One can see this unity fragmentarily in personalities in whom grace is effective, in the secular as well as the religious realm. In contrast to such "symbols of reunion," the existential disruption of dynamics and form is obvious. Under the control of *hubris* and concupiscence, man is driven in all directions without any definite aim and content. His dynamics are distorted into a formless urge for self-transcendence. It is not the new form which attracts the self-transcendence of the person; the dynamics has become an aim in itself. One can speak of the "temptation of the new," which in itself is a necessary element in all creative self-actualization but which in distortion sacrifices the creative for the new. Nothing real is created if the form is lacking, for nothing is real without form.

Yet form without dynamics is equally destructive. If a form is abstracted from the dynamics in which it is created and is imposed on the dynamics to which it does not belong, it becomes external law. It is oppressive and produces either legalism without creativity or the rebellious outbreaks of dynamic forces leading to chaos and often, in reaction, to stronger ways of suppression. Such experiences belong to man's predicament in individual as well as in social life, in religion as well as in culture. There is a continuous flight from law to chaos and from chaos to law. There is a continuous breaking of vitality by form and of form by vitality. But, if the one side disappears, the other does also. Dynamics, vitality, and the drive to form-breaking end in chaos and emptiness. They lose themselves in their separation from form. And form, structure, and law end in rigidity and emptiness. They lose themselves in their separation from dynamics.

This includes the basic criticism of all doctrines of man which describe man's essential nature either in terms of mere dynamics or in terms of mere form. We have already pointed to some of them in connection with the doctrine of concupiscence. If man is understood as essentially unlimited libido or unlimited will to power, the basis for such understanding is not man's essential nature but his state of existential estrangement. The inability to reach a form in which the dynamics of man's nature are preliminarily or lastingly satisfied is an expression of man's estrangement from himself and the essential unity of dynamics and form. The same criticism must be applied to interpretations of human nature which deprive him of the dynamics in his being by reducing his true being to a system of logical, moral, and aesthetic forms to which he must conform. Common-sense philosophies, as well as some rationalistic and idealistic doctrines of man, eliminate the dynamics in man's self-realization. Creativity is replaced by subjection to law—a characteristic of man in estrangement.

Both types of the doctrine of man—the dynamic and the formal—describe man's existential predicament. This is their truth and the limit of their truth.

c) The separation of individualization from participation.—Life individualizes in all its forms; at the same time, mutual participation of being in "being" maintains the unity of being. The two poles are interdependent. The more individualized a being is, the more it is able to participate. Man as the completely individualized being participates in the world in its totality through perception, imagination, and action. In principle, there are no limits to his participation, since he is a completely centered self. In the state of estrangement man is shut within himself and cut off from participation. At the same time, he falls under the power of objects which tend to make him into a mere object without a self. If subjectivity separates itself from objectivity, the objects swallow the empty shell of subjectivity.

This situation has been described sociologically and psychologically. These descriptions have shown the interdependence of the loneliness of the individual and his submergence in the collective in a convincing way. However, they are directed toward a particular historical situation, predominantly our own. They give the impression that the situation to which they point is historically and sociologically conditioned and would change basically with a change in conditions. Theology must join existentialism in showing the universally human character of loneliness in interdependence with submergence in the collective. It is true that special situations reveal more sharply special elements in man's existential situation. They reveal them, but they do not create them. The danger of depersonalization or "objectivization" (becoming a thing) is most outspoken in Western industrial society. But there are dangers of the same character in all societies; for the separation of individualization from participation is a mark of estrangement generally. These dangers belong to the structures of destruction and are grounded in the level of evil in all history.

This situation is also mirrored in those doctrines of man which claim to describe man's essential nature but which give a true account only about man's estrangement. Isolated subjectivity appears in idealistic epistemologies which reduce man to a cognitive subject (*ens cogitans*), who perceives, analyzes, and controls reality. The act of knowing is deprived of any participation of the total subject in the total object. There is no *eros* in the way in which the subject approaches the object and in which the object gives itself to the subject. On some levels of abstraction this is necessary; but if it determines the cognitive approach as a whole, it is a symptom of estrangement. And, since man is a part of his world, he himself becomes a mere object among objects. He becomes a part of the physically calculable whole, thus becoming a thoroughly calculable object himself. This is the case whether the psychological level is explained physiologically and chemically or whether it is described in terms of independent psychological mechanisms. In both cases a theoretical objectivation is carried through which can be and is being used for the practical dealing with men as though they were mere objects. The situation of estrangement is mirrored in both the theoretical and the practical encounter with man as a mere object. Both are "structures of self-destruction," i.e., basic sources of evil.

3. FINITUDE AND ESTRANGEMENT

a) Death, finitude, and guilt.—Estranged from the ultimate power of being, man is determined by his finitude. He is given over to his natural fate. He came from nothing, and he returns to nothing. He is under the domination of death and is driven by the anxiety of having to die. This, in fact, is the first answer to the question about the relation of sin and death. In conformity with biblical religion, it asserts that man is naturally mortal. Immortality as a natural quality of man is not a Christian doctrine, though it is possibly a Platonic doctrine. But even Plato has Socrates put a question mark on the very arguments for the immortality of the soul which Socrates develops in the discussions prior to his death. Certainly, the nature of the eternal life which he attributes to the soul has little resemblance to the popular beliefs of many Christians about the "hereafter." Plato speaks of the participation of the soul in the eternal realm of essences (ideas), of its fall from and possible return to this realm—though not a realm in any spatial or temporal sense. In the biblical story of paradise a quite different interpretation of the relation of the Fall and death is given. The biblical symbols are even farther removed from the popular image of immortality. According to the Genesis account, man comes from dust and returns to dust. He has immortality only as long as he is allowed to eat from the tree of life, the tree which carries the divine food or the food of eternal life. The symbolism is obvious. Participation in the eternal makes man eternal; separation from the eternal leaves man in his natural finitude. It was therefore in line with these ideas that the early Church Fathers called the sacramental food of the Lord's Supper the "medicine of immortality," and that the Eastern church let the message of the Christ focus on his resurrection as the moment in which eternal life is provided for those who are otherwise left to their natural mortality. In estrangement man is left to his finite nature of having to die. Sin does not produce death but gives to death the power which is conquered only in participation in the eternal. The idea that the "Fall" has physically changed the cellular or psychological structure of man (and nature?) is absurd and unbiblical.

If man is left to his "having to die," the essential anxiety about non-being is transformed into the horror of death. Anxiety about non-being is present in everything finite. It is consciously or unconsciously effective in the whole process of living. Like the beating of the heart, it is always present, although one is not always aware of it. It belongs to the potential state of dreaming innocence, as well as to the contested and decided unity with God as expressed in the picture of Jesus as the Christ. The dramatic description of the anxiety of Jesus in having to die confirms the universal character of the relation of finitude and anxiety.

Under the conditions of estrangement, anxiety has a different character, brought on by the element of guilt. The loss of one's potential eternity is experienced as something for which one is responsible in spite of its universal tragic actuality. Sin is the sting of death, not its physical cause. It transforms the anxious awareness of one's having to die into the painful realization of a lost eternity. For this reason the anxiety about having to die can be connected with the desire to get rid of one's self. One desires annihilation in order to escape death in its nature, not only as end, but also as guilt. Under the condition of estrangement, anxiety about death is more than anxiety about annihilation. It makes death an evil, a structure of destruction.

The transformation of essential finitude into existential evil is a general characteristic of the state of estrangement. It has been depicted most recently in both Christian and non-Christian analyses of the human situation, recently and very powerfully in existentialist literature. Such descriptions are acceptable—and extremely important—for theology, if the sharp distinction between finitude and estrangement, as illustrated in the analysis of death, is maintained. If this is not done, the description, no matter how much valuable material it provides, must be revised in the light of the doctrine of creation and the distinction between essential and existential being.

b) *Estrangement, time, and space.*—No description of the structures of evil can be exhaustive. It is an infinite task. The pages of the world's literature are filled with it in every time and place. New discoveries about the workings of evil are continuously made. Biblical literature is full of them, but so also is the literature of other religions and the works of secular culture. Theology must be conscious of this universal awareness of forms of evil. It cannot enumerate them, but it can and must show some basic structures. As structures of evil, they are structures of self-destruction. They are based on the structures of finitude; but they add the destructive elements and transform them, as guilt transforms the anxiety of death.

The categorical nature of finitude, including time, space, causality, and substance, is valid as structure in the whole of creation. But the function of the categories of finitude is changed under the conditions of existence. In the categories, the unity of being and non-being in all finite beings is manifest. Therefore, they produce anxiety; but they can be affirmed by courage, if the predominance of being over non-being is experienced. In the state of estrangement, the relation to the ultimate power of being is lost. In that state, the categories control existence and produce a double reaction toward them—resistance and despair.

When time is experienced without the "eternal now" through the presence of the power of being itself, it is known as mere transitoriness without actual presence. It is seen—as the myths concerning the gods of time indicate—as a demonic power, destroying what it has created. The attempts of man to resist it are of no avail. Man tries to prolong the small stretch of time given to him; he tries to fill the moment with as many transitory things as possible; he tries to create for himself a memory in a future which is not his; he imagines a continuation of his life after the end of his time and an endlessness without eternity.

These are forms of human resistance against the ultimate threat of non-being implied in the category of time. The breakdown of this resistance in its many forms is one element in the structure of despair. It is not the experience of time as such which produces despair; rather it is defeat in the resistance against time. In itself, this resistance stems from man's essential belonging to the eternal, his exclusion from it in the state of estrangement, and his desire to transform the transitory moments of his time into a lasting presence. His existential unwillingness to accept his temporality makes time a demonic structure of destruction for him.

When space is experienced without the "eternal here" as the presence of the power of being itself, it is experienced as spatial contingency, i.e., without a necessary place to which man belongs. It is seen as the result of the play of divine-demonic powers (Heraclitus) which disregard any inner relation of the person to the physical, sociological, or psychological "place on which he stands." Man tries to resist this situation. He tries in an absolute sense to make a definite place his own. In all longing for a final "home," this desire is effective. But he does not succeed; he remains a "pilgrim on earth," and finally "his place does not know him any longer" (Job). This also is the outcome if he tries to make his own as many spaces as possible, whether by actual or by imaginary imperialism. He replaces the dimension of the "eternal here" by the dimension of the "universal here." He tries to resist the spatial "beside each other," which includes his finitude, and he is defeated and thrown into the despair of ultimate uprootedness.

Similar observations could be made about other categories, e.g., about man's attempt to make himself into an absolute cause in resistance to the endless chain of causes in which he is one among others, about his attempt to give to himself an absolute substance in resistance to the vanishing of the substance along with the accidents. These attempts are expressions of man's awareness of his potential infinity. But they necessarily fail if they are attempted without the presence of the ground of all causal dependence and all accidental changes. Without the power of being itself, man cannot resist the element of non-being in both causality and substance, and his failure to resist is another element in the structure of despair.

c) Estrangement, suffering, and loneliness.—The conflicts in the ontological polarities and the transformation of the categories of finitude under the conditions of estrangement have consequences for man's predicament in all directions. Two outstanding examples of these consequences are discussed here—suffering and loneliness. The former concerns man in himself; the latter, man in relation to others. These two cannot be separated from each other; they are interdependent, though distinguishable.

Suffering, like death, is an element of finitude. It is not removed but is transformed into blessedness in the state of dreaming innocence. Under the conditions of existence, man is cut off from this blessedness, and suffering lays hold of him in a destructive way. Suffering becomes a structure of destruction—an evil. It is decisive for the understanding of Christianity and the great religions of the East, especially Buddhism, that suffering as an element of essential finitude is distinguished from suffering as an element of existential estrangement. If, as in Buddhism, this distinction is not made, finitude and evil are identified. Salvation becomes salvation from finitude and from the suffering it implies. But it is not—as it is in Christianity—salvation from the estrangement which transforms suffering into a structure of destruction. The Buddhist interpretation of suffering is right to the extent that it derives suffering from the will to be. Suffering is therefore overcome by the self-negation of the will's desire to be something particular. In Christianity the demand is made to accept suffering as an element of finitude with an ultimate courage and thereby to overcome that suffering which is dependent on existential estrangement, which is mere destruction. Christianity knows that such a victory over destructive suffering is only partly possible in time and space. But whether this fragmentary victory is fought for or not makes all the difference between Western and Eastern cultures, as a comparison shows. It changes the valuation of the individual, of personality, of community, and of history. It has, in fact, determined the historical destiny of mankind.

The distinction between suffering as an expression of finitude and as a result of estrangement is valid, in spite of the fact that it never can be concretely affirmed because of the ambiguity which characterizes life as life. But it is possible to speak of the type of suffering in which meaning can be experienced, in contrast, for example, to meaningless suffering. Suffering is meaningful to the extent that it calls for protection and healing in the being which is attacked by pain. It can show the limits and the potentialities of a living being. Whether it does so or not is dependent both on the objective character of suffering and on the way in which it is taken by the suffering subject. There are forms of suffering which destroy the possibility of the subject's acting as subject, as in cases of psychotic destruction, dehumanizing external conditions, or a radical reduction in bodily resistance. Existence is full of instances in which no meaning can be found in suffering on the part of the suffering subject. Such a situation, of course, is not implied in essential being. It is based on the transition from essence to existence and on the conflicts which follow from the self-actualization of being in encounters with beings. It is implied in existence.

One of the causes of meaningless suffering—indeed, the main cause —is the "aloneness" of the individual being, his desire to overcome it by union with other beings, and the hostility which results from the rejection of this desire. Here again it is necessary to distinguish essential and existential structures of aloneness. Every living being is structurally centered; man has a completely centered self. This centeredness cuts him off from the whole of reality which is not identified with himself. He is alone in his world and the more so, the more he is conscious of himself as himself. On the other hand, his complete centeredness enables him to participate in his world without limits; and love, as the dynamic power of life, drives him toward such participation. In the state of essential being the participation is limited by finitude, but participation is not prevented by rejection. The structure of finitude is good in itself, but under the conditions of estrangement it becomes a structure of destruction. Being alone in essential finitude is an expression of man's complete centeredness and could be called "solitude." It is the condition for the relation to the other one. Only he who is able to have solitude is able to have communion. For in solitude man experiences the dimension of the ultimate, the true basis for communion among those who are alone. In existential estrangement man is cut off from the dimensions of the ultimate and is left alone—in loneliness. This loneliness, however, is intolerable. It drives man to a type of participation in which he surrenders his lonely self to the "collective."

But in this surrender the individual is accepted not by any other individual but only by that to which they have all surrendered their potential solitude, that is, the spirit of the collective. Therefore, the individual continues to seek for the other one and is rejected, in part or in full; for the other one is also a lonely individual, unable to have communion because he is unable to have solitude. Such rejection is the source of much hostility not only against those who reject one but also against one's self. In this way the essential structure of solitude and communion is distorted by existential estrangement into a source of infinite suffering. Destruction of others and self-destruction are interdependent in the dialectics of loneliness.

If the distinction between essential solitude and existential loneliness is not maintained, ultimate unity is possible only by the annihilation of the lonely individual and through his disappearance in an undifferentiated substance. The solution aspired to in radical mysticism is analogous to the answer to the problem of suffering given in Buddhism. There is no loneliness in the ultimate; but neither is there solitude or communion, because the centered self of the individual has been dissolved. This comparison shows how decisive for the Christian understanding of evil and salvation is the distinction between essential solitude and existential loneliness.

d) Estrangement, doubt, and meaninglessness.—Finitude includes doubt. The true is the whole (Hegel). But no finite being has the whole; therefore, it is an expression of the acceptance of his finitude that he accepts the fact that doubt belongs to his essential being. Even dreaming innocence implies doubt. Therefore, the serpent in the myth of the paradise story could evoke the doubt of man.

Essential doubt is present in the methodological doubt of science as well as in the uncertainty about one's self, one's world, and the ultimate meaning of both. No proof is needed to show that, without the radical questioning of everything, there is no cognitive approach to an encountered reality. The question indicates both a having (without which no question would be possible) and a not-having (without which no question would be necessary). This situation of essential doubt is given to man even in the state of estrangement and makes it possible for him to analyze and control reality to the extent that he is willing to use it honestly and sacrificially.

But finitude also includes uncertainty in every other respect; it is an expression of the general insecurity of the finite being, the contingency of his being at all, the fact that he is not by himself but is "thrown into being" (Heidegger), the lack of a necessary place and a necessary presence. This insecurity also appears in the choices in personal relations and in other parts of encountered reality. It appears in the indefiniteness of feeling and in the risk in every decision. Finally, it appears in the doubt about one's self and one's world as such; it appears as the doubt or uncertainty about being as being.

All these forms of insecurity and uncertainty belong to man's essential finitude, to the goodness of the creative in so far as it is created. In the state of mere potentiality, insecurity and uncertainty are present, but they are accepted in the power of the dimension of the eternal. In this dimension there is an ultimate security or certainty which does not cancel out the preliminary insecurities and uncertainties of finitude (including the anxiety of their awareness). Rather it takes them into itself with the courage to accept one's finitude.

If in the state of estrangement the dimension of the ultimate is shut off, the situation changes. Insecurity becomes absolute and drives toward a despair about the possibility of being at all. Doubt becomes absolute and drives toward a despairing refusal to accept any finite truth. Both together produce the experience that the structure of finitude has become a structure of existential destruction.

The destructive character of existential insecurity and doubt is manifest in the way man tries to escape despair. He tries to make absolute a finite security or a finite certainty. The threat of a breakdown leads to the establishment of defenses, some of which are brutal, some fanatical, some dishonest, and all insufficient and destructive; for there is no security and certainty within finitude. The destructive force may be directed against those who represent the threat to false security and certainty, especially against those who compete or contradict. War and persecution are partly dependent on these dialectics. If, however, the defenses prove to be insufficient, the destructive force is directed against the subject himself. He is thrown into restlessness, emptiness, cynicism, and the experience of meaninglessness. And it may well be that, in order to escape this extreme, he negates his doubt not by a real or imaginary answer but by indifference toward any question or answer. In this way he destroys his genuine humanity and becomes a cog within the great machine of work and pleasure. He is deprived of meaning, even in the form of suffering under meaninglessness. Not even the meaningfulness of a serious question of meaning is left for him.

In these descriptions it can be observed that the distinction between sin and evil is only partly valid. In evil as the self-destructive consequence of sin, sin itself is present. The element of responsibility is not lacking in structures of destruction, such as meaningless suffering, loneliness, cynical doubt, meaninglessness, or despair. On the other hand, each of these structures is dependent on the universal state of estrangement and its self-destructive consequences. From this point of view, it is justifiable to speak of "sin" in the one context and of "evil" in the other. It is a difference more of focus than of content.

Another question has come to the fore in contemporary sociological and psychological analyses. It is the question of how far the structures of destruction are universally human and how far they are historically conditioned. The answer is that their historical appearance is possible only because of their universal, structural presence. Estrangement is a quality of the structure of existence, but the way in which estrangement is predominantly manifest is a matter of history. There are always structures of destruction in history, but they are possible only because there are structures of finitude which can be transformed into structures of estrangement. There are many sociological and existentialist analyses of man in industrial society which point to self-loss and world-loss, to mechanization and objectification, to loneliness and surrender to the collective, to the experience of emptiness and meaninglessness. These analyses are true as far as they go, but they are fallacious if in our period of history they derive the evil of man's predicament from the structure of industrial society. Such a derivation implies the belief that changes in the structure of our society would, as such, change man's existential predicament. All utopianism has this character; its main mistake is in not distinguishing man's existential situation from its manifestation in different historical periods. There are structures of destruction in all periods, and they provide many analogies with the particular structures of our period. Man's estrangement from his essential being is the universal character of existence. It is inexhaustibly productive of particular evils in every period.

Structures of destruction are not the only mark of existence. They are counterbalanced by structures of healing and reunion of the estranged. But this ambiguity of life is not a reason for the utopian derivation of the evils of a period from the structures of this period without reference to the situation of universal estrangement.

4. THE MEANING OF DESPAIR AND ITS SYMBOLS

a) Despair and the problem of suicide.—The structures of evil we have described drive man into the state of "despair." In several places we pointed to elements of despair but not to the nature of despair as a whole. The latter task must be undertaken in systematic theology. Despair is usually discussed as a psychological problem or as a problem of ethics. It certainly is both; but it is more than this: it is the final index of man's predicament; it is the boundary line beyond which man cannot go. In despair, not in death, man has come to the end of his possibilities. The word itself means "without hope" and expresses the feeling of a situation from which there is "no exit" (Sartre). In German the word *Verzweiflung* connects despair with doubt (*Zweifel*). The syllable *ver-* indicates a doubt without a possible answer. The most impressive description of the situation of despair has been given by Kierkegaard in *Sickness unto Death,* where "death" means beyond possible healing. And Paul points in a similar way to a sorrow which is the sorrow of this world and leads to death.

Despair is the state of inescapable conflict. It is the conflict, on the one hand, between what one potentially is and therefore ought to be and, on the other hand, what one actually is in the combination of freedom and destiny. The pain of despair is the agony of being responsible for the loss of the meaning of one's existence and of being unable to recover it. One is shut up in one's self and in the conflict with one's self. One cannot escape, because one cannot escape from one's self. It is out of this situation that the question arises whether suicide may be a way of getting rid of one's self. There can be no doubt that suicide has a much wider significance than seems warranted by the comparatively small number of actual suicidal acts. First of all, there is a suicidal tendency in life generally, the longing for rest without conflict. The human desire for intoxication is a consequence of this longing (compare Freud's doctrine of the death instinct and its evaluation above). Second, in every moment of intolerable, insuperable, and meaningless pain there is the desire to escape the pain by getting rid of one's self. Third, the situation of despair is most conspicuously a situation in which the desire to get rid of one's self is awake and the image of suicide appears in a most tempting way. Fourth, there are situations in which the unconscious will to life is undermined and a psychological suicide takes place in terms of non-resistance to threatening annihilation. Fifth, whole cultures preach the self-negation of the will, not in terms of physical or psychological suicide, but in terms of the emptying of life of all finite contents so that the entrance into the ultimate identity is possible.

In view of these facts, the question of the self-negation of life should be taken more seriously than Christian theology usually does. The external act of suicide should not be singled out for special moral and religious condemnation. Such a practice is based on the superstitious idea that suicide definitively excludes the operation of saving grace. At the same time, the inner suicidal trends in everyone should be considered as an expression of human estrangement.

The decisive and theologically involved question is: Why cannot suicide be considered an escape from despair? Obviously, there is no problem for those who believe that such an escape is impossible because life goes on after death under essentially the same conditions as before, including the categories of finitude. But if death is taken seriously, one cannot deny that suicide removes the conditions of despair on the level of finitude. One can ask, however, whether this level is the only one or whether the element of guilt in despair points to the dimension of the ultimate. If this is affirmed—and Christianity certainly must affirm it—suicide is no final escape. It does not release us from the dimension of the ultimate and unconditional. One could express this in a somehow mythological way by saying that no personal problem is a matter of mere transitoriness but has eternal roots and demands a solution in relation to the eternal. Suicide (whether external, psychological, or metaphysical) is a successful attempt to escape the situation of despair on the temporal level. But it is not successful in the dimension of the eternal. The problem of salvation transcends the temporal level, and the experience of despair itself points to this truth.

b) The symbol of the "wrath of God."—The experience of despair is reflected in the symbol of the "wrath of God." Christian theologians have both used and criticized the term. Criticism has usually recalled that in paganism the concept of the "anger of the gods" presupposes the idolatrous idea of a finite god whose emotions can be aroused by other finite beings. Such a concept obviously contradicts the divinity of the divine and its unconditional character. Therefore, the concept has to be reinterpreted or completely abandoned in Christian thought. The latter alternative was taken by Albrecht Ritschl, not only in the name of the divinity of the divine, but also in the name of the divine love which he believed to be the true nature of God. If one speaks of the "wrath" of God, one seems to create a split in God between love and wrath. God is, so to speak, caught in his wrath, and then his love must find a way out of this conflict. The atoning work of Christ is then construed as the solution which enables God to forgive what has aroused his wrath, because in the death of Christ his wrath is satisfied. Such an approach, which was frequently elaborated in quantitative and mechanical categories, indeed violated the majesty of God. Ritschl therefore interpreted the New Testament passages in which the wrath of God is mentioned in such a way as to point to the ultimate judgment. The wrath of God is an expression of the negative side of the final judgment. One must ask, however, whether the experience of despair does not justify the use of the symbol "wrath of God" to express an element in the relationship between God and man. One may refer to Luther, who showed an existential approach to the problem when he said: "As you believe him, so you have him." For those who are aware of their own estrangement from God, God is the threat of ultimate destruction. His face takes on demonic traits. However, those who are reconciled to him realize that, although their experience of the wrath of God was genuine, it was not the experience of a God other than the one to whom they are reconciled. Rather their experience was the way in which the God of love acted in relation to them. The divine love stands against all that which is against love, leaving it to its self-destruction, in order to save those who are destroyed; for, since that which is against love occurs in persons, it is the person which falls into self-destruction. This is the only way in which love can operate in the one who rejects love. In showing any man the self-destructive consequences of his rejection of love, love acts according to its own nature, although he who experiences it does so as a threat to his being. He perceives God as the God of wrath, rightly so in preliminary terms, wrongly so in ultimate terms. But the theoretical knowledge that his experience of God as the God of wrath is not the final experience of God does not remove the reality of God as a threat to his being and nothing but a threat.(Only the acceptance of forgiveness can transform the image of the wrathful God into the ultimately valid image of the God of love.

c) The symbol of "condemnation."—The experience of despair is also expressed in the symbol of "condemnation." Usually one speaks of "eternal condemnation." But this is a theologically untenable combination of words. God alone is eternal. Those who participate in the divine eternity and in the limitation of finitude have conquered the despair expressed in the experience of condemnation. In the theologically precise sense of the word, eternity is the opposite of condemnation. But if "eternal" is understood as "endless," one would ascribe endless condemnation to that which by its very nature has an end, namely, finite man. Man's time comes to an end with himself. Therefore, one should eliminate the term "eternal condemnation" from the theological vocabulary. Instead, one should speak of condemnation as removal from the eternal. This seems to be implied in the term "eternal death," which certainly cannot mean everlasting death, since death has no duration. The experience of separation from one's eternity is the state of despair. It points beyond the limits of temporality and to the situation of being bound to the divine life without being united with it in the central act of personal love. Neither experience nor language allows us to say more about it. For the negative can be experienced and spoken of only in union with the positive. Both for time and for eternity, one must say that even in the state of separation God is creatively working in us—even if his creativity takes the way of destruction. Man is never cut off from the ground of being, not even in the state of condemnation.

E. THE QUEST FOR THE NEW BEING AND THE MEANING OF "CHRIST"

1. Existence as Fate or the Bondage of the Will

In every act of existential self-realization, freedom and destiny are united. Existence is always both fact and act. From this it follows that no act within the context of existential estrangement can overcome existential estrangement. Destiny keeps freedom in bondage without eliminating it. This is expressed in the doctrine of the "bondage of the will" as developed by Luther in his fight with Erasmus. Before this it was expressed by Augustine against Pelagius and, before that, by Paul against the Judaists. In these three instances and in many others the meaning of theological anti-Pelagianism has been misunderstood by being confused with philosophical determinism. The anti-Pelagian theologians have been accused of surrendering human freedom and making man into an object among objects. Sometimes their language (even in Paul) approximates this "Manichaean" error. And some theologians cannot be defended against such an accusation. But the anti-Pelagian emphasis does not necessarily lead to Manichaean tendencies; for the doctrine of the bondage of the will presupposes the freedom of the will. Only what is essentially free can come under existential bondage. In our experience "bondage of the will" is a term that can apply only to man. Nature, too, has spontaneity and centeredness, but it does not have freedom. Therefore, it cannot fall under the bondage of the will. Only man, because he is finite freedom, is open to the compulsions of existential estrangement.

On this level Erasmus is right when he quotes biblical passages against Luther's doctrine of the bondage of the will. He points to that moral responsibility which makes man, man. Yet this was not denied, either by Luther or by the other representatives of the concept of the bondage of the will. They did not deny that *man,* a being with finite freedom, is saved; they believed that he who is saved is a sinner, namely, the one who shows this by his freedom to contradict his essential nature. Grace does not create a being who is unconnected with the one who receives grace. Grace does not destroy essential freedom; but it does what freedom under the conditions of existence cannot do, namely, it reunites the estranged.

Nevertheless, the bondage of the will is a universal fact. It is the inability of man to break through his estrangement. In spite of the power of his finite freedom, he is unable to achieve the reunion with God. In the realm of finite relations, all decisions are expressions of man's essential freedom. But they do not bring reunion with God; they remain in the realm of "civil justice," of moral and legal norms. But even these decisions, despite the ambiguity of all the structures of life, are related to the unambiguous and ultimate. Man, in relation to God, cannot do anything without him. He must receive in order to act. New being precedes new acting. The tree produces the fruits, not the fruits the tree. Man cannot control his compulsions except by the power of that which happens to him in the root of these compulsions. This psychological truth is also a religious truth, the truth of the "bondage of the will." Attempts to overcome estrangement within the power of one's estranged existence lead to hard toil and tragic failure. They are without joy. Therefore, for Luther, the law is not fulfilled unless it is fulfilled joyfully. For the law is not strange to our being. It is our being itself, expressed in the form of commandment. And fulfilment of one's being is joy. Paul speaks of the obedience of the child in contrast to the obedience of the slave. But, in order to act like children, we must have received childhood; the union with God must have been re-established. Only a New Being can produce a new action.

2. Ways of Self-salvation and Their Failure

a) *Self-salvation and religion.*—The principle that being precedes acting implies a basic criticism of the history of religion, to the extent that it is the history of man's attempts and failures to save himself. Although religion belongs to the functions of man's spiritual life and is therefore an expression of life generally, uniting essential and existential elements, we must refer to it in the present context which deals only with existence. For religion is not only a function of life; it is also the place where life receives the conqueror of the ambiguities of life, the divine Spirit. Therefore, it is the sphere in which the quest for the New Being appears over against the split between essential and existential being. The question of salvation can be asked only if salvation is already at work, no matter how fragmentarily. Pure despair—the state without hope—is unable to seek beyond itself. The quest for the New Being presupposes the presence of the New Being, as the search for truth presupposes the presence of truth. This necessary circle restates what has been said in the methodological part about the interdependence of all parts of the theological system. The theological circle follows from the non-deductive, existential character of theology. For our present purpose, this means that the concept of religion must be commented on prior to its systematic treatment. The quest for the Christ as well as the attempts at self-salvation appear in the religious sphere. It is equally wrong to identify religion with revelation, just as it is wrong to identify religion with the attempt at self-salvation. Religion, like all life, is ambiguous. On the basis of revelatory experiences, religion turns to self-salvation. It distorts what it has received and fails in what it tries to achieve. This is the tragedy of religion.

b) Legalistic ways of self-salvation.—Most conspicuous and important for the history of religion are the legalistic ways of self-salvation.
Judaism is right in contending that obedience to the law is not legalism. The law is, first of all, a divine gift; it shows to man his essential
nature, his true relationship to God, other men, and himself. Within
existential estrangement it makes man's true nature manifest. But it
does so in terms of commandments, just because man is estranged from
what he ought to be. This is the possibility and the temptation of legalism. It is an almost irresistible temptation. Man, seeing what he ought
to be, driven by the anxiety of losing himself, believing in his strength
to actualize his essential being, disregarding the bondage of the will,
tries to attain again what he has lost. But this situation of estrangement, in which the law becomes commandment, is just the situation in
which the law cannot be fulfilled. The conditions of existence simultaneously make the commanding law necessary and its fulfilment impossible. This is true of every particular commandment and of the all-
embracing law, the law of love. Necessarily, love has become commandment in the state of estrangement. But love cannot be commanded—
even if it is not misunderstood as emotion. It cannot be commanded,
because it is the power of that reunion which precedes and fulfils the
command before it is given.

Whenever attempted, legalism as a way of self-salvation has come to
catastrophe. In all forms of legalism, something which is good, namely,
in agreement with man's essential nature, becomes distorted. All forms
of legalism are based ultimately on a revelatory experience, received
and taken seriously. Their greatness is their unconditional seriousness
(which is manifest even in the obedience to the civil and conventional
laws). Their distortion is their claim to overcome the state of estrangement by their serious obedience to the commanding law.

The failure of legalism to achieve the reunion of the separated can
lead to an attitude of compromising half-seriousness, to a rejection of
the law, to despair, or—through despair—to the quest for a New Being.
In the last instance, that which is asked for even the radical seriousness
under the law cannot attain.

c) Ascetic ways of self-salvation.—Between legalism and its opposite,
mysticism, stands asceticism. An ascetic element is to be found in all
forms of legalism. In order to avoid the lawlessness of concupiscence,
the ascetic tries to extinguish desire completely by eliminating as many
objects of possible desire as he can within the limits of finite existence.

Here again a truth is distorted by the attempt to use it as a way to self-salvation.

The term "asceticism" is used in different ways. It designates self-restriction in connection with obedience to law. As such, it is a necessary element in every act of moral self-realization. It puts limits to the endlessness of libido and the will to power and turns them to an acceptance of one's finitude. As such, it is an implement of wisdom and a demand of love.

Asceticism is also a restriction which is not demanded in itself but is used as a means of self-discipline when self-restriction is objectively demanded. Such asceticism is admissible if it is a disciplinary exercise and does not claim to be more. It is, however, always in danger of being valued as a means to self-salvation. The voluntary putting-aside of something objectively good in itself often appears as a victory over estrangement.

There is a similar danger in using ascetic restriction in relation to one finite good in order to attain another finite good. This is "inner worldly asceticism" and is exemplified in the Puritan attitude toward work, pleasure, accumulation of money, etc. These qualities had their reward in the technical and economic control of nature and society, and this has been valued as an expression of divine blessing. Although, doctrinally, ascetic self-restriction does not earn the divine blessing, psychologically the ascetic self-control of the Puritan is inevitably turned into a cause of divine blessing. In this way, self-salvation through ascetic acts crept into Protestant churches, even though they are doctrinally based on the most radical rejection of self-salvation.

The main form of asceticism, which could be called "ontological asceticism," is based on the ontological devaluation of finite being. Finitude should not be, because it contradicts being itself. Finitude and Fall are identical, and the tragic state of finite reality is beyond salvation. The only way to salvation is through the complete negation of finite reality, emptying one's self of the manifold contents of the encountered world. The main ascetic ways of self-salvation as elaborated historically are usually part of a mystical type of religion in which self-salvation is attempted through mystical evaluation beyond finite reality.

Ascetic methods of self-salvation fail in so far as they try to force the reunion with the infinite by conscious acts of self-negation. But the objects of concupiscence in human nature do not actually disappear; they are still present in the form of repression. Therefore, they often reappear in the form of overengrossing imagination or in such transformations as the will to domination, fanaticism, and sado-masochistic or suicidal tendencies. According to medieval art and literature, the demonic is most surely manifested in the medieval ascetics.

As an element in the processes of life, asceticism is necessary; as an attempt at self-salvation, asceticism is a dangerous distortion and a failure.

d) Mystical ways of self-salvation.—Ordinarily, the ontological form of asceticism appears in mysticism. Therefore, we must now deal with the mystical attempts at self-salvation. Since Protestant theologians have often accused mysticism of being *only* a way to self-salvation, it is necessary to distinguish the different meanings of the term "mystical." "Mystical" is, first of all, a category which characterizes the divine as being present in experience. In this sense, the mystical is the heart of every religion as religion. A religion which cannot say "God himself is present" becomes a system of moral or doctrinal rules which are not religious, even if they are derived from originally revelatory sources. Mysticism, or the "felt presence of God," is a category essential to the nature of religion and has nothing to do with self-salvation.

But self-salvation is evident if one tries to reach reunion through bodily and mental exercises. Much Eastern and parts of Western mysticism do have this character. In this sense, mysticism is largely, though not fully, an attempt at self-salvation, at trying to transcend all realms of finite being in order to unite the finite being with the infinite. But this attempt, like the other attempts at self-salvation, is a failure. A real union of the mystic with God is never reached. But, even if it were reached, it would not overcome the estrangement of ordinary existence. Long stretches of "dryness of the soul" follow moments of ecstasy, and the predicament of men generally is not changed because the conditions of existence are left untouched.

However, classical mysticism denies the possibility of self-salvation at the last stage of ecstasy. In spite of all the preparations, the ecstatic reunion with the ultimate cannot be forced when this point has been reached. It must be given, yet might not be given at all. This decisive limit to the self-saving methods of mysticism should curb the often very summary and unrefined criticism of the great mystics by Protestant theologians, Ritschlian as well as neo-orthodox.

If theologians paid more attention to the limits seen by the mystics themselves, they would have to give a more positive evaluation of this great tradition. One would then understand that there is something one could call "baptized mysticism," in which the mystical experience depends on the appearance of the new reality and does not attempt to produce it. The form of this mysticism is concrete, in contrast to the abstract mysticism of the classical mystical systems. It follows Paul's experience of being "*in* Christ," namely, in the spiritual power which is Christ. In principle, such mysticism is beyond the attitude of self-salvation, although it is not protected against actual relapses; for self-salvation is a temptation in all religious forms, and relapses appear in the midst of Christianity.

e) Sacramental, doctrinal, emotional ways of self-salvation.—To the legalistic, ascetic, and mystical ways of self-salvation can be added the sacramental, the doctrinal, and the emotional.

Although the sacramental way is more characteristic of the Roman Catholic church and the doctrinal way more characteristic of the Protestant church, especially the Lutheran churches, it is possible to discuss both ways together. There is so much doctrinal self-salvation in Roman Catholicism and so much sacramental self-salvation in Lutheran Protestantism that a separate treatment would be inappropriate. In both cases a special manifestation of the New Being in visual or verbal form is distorted into a ritual or intellectual work which conquers existential estrangement through its very performance. Salvation is dependent upon the sacramental act performed by the priest and participated in by the Christian; or it is dependent upon the true doctrines formulated by the church and accepted by the Christian. In Roman Catholicism the sacramental work is justified because the Roman church is a synthesis of salvation by God and self-salvation. In Protestantism the Pelagian element of self-salvation was removed, but it nevertheless returned both in orthodoxy and in pietism (fundamentalism and revivalism). Classical orthodoxy established a kind of "sacramentalism of the pure doctrine." Under the title "obedience to the word of God," obedience was asked to the letter of the Bible, and, since the meaning of the Bible is not obvious, obedience to a special interpretation of the Bible by a special, historically dated theology was demanded (and is demanded in present-day fundamentalism). In many cases, especially in a period in which critical consciousness developed, this led to an intellectual asceticism or to the sacrifice of man's critical power. This demand is analogous to that made in monastic or Puritan asceticism, where all vital powers are sacrificed.

Having shown the interdependence of the sacramental and doctrinal in theory and in fact, it is still possible to delineate their shortcomings separately. Sacramental self-salvation is the distortion of sacramental receptivity. The sacramental presence of the divine, expressed in ways which go far beyond the so-called sacraments, is itself in opposition to self-salvation. But in religious actualization in rites, elements of self-salvation can enter the procedures and distort their original meaning. The mere performance of the accepted rites or the mere participation in a sacramental act is considered to have saving power. The sacrament is given, and, as such, it is understood to negate self-salvation. But the way in which it is used opens wide the door for a self-saving attitude. The anxious question of whether or not one has performed what one should perform or whether one has proceeded with the right form and with the right attitude shows that reunion with the divine source of the sacramental act has not been reached. Sacramental self-salvation is not only a highly dialectical concept; it is also an actual impossibility. It can never bring about a reunion with God.

The same is true of doctrinal self-salvation. In Lutheran Protestantism the phrase "justification by faith" was partly responsible for the distortion of doctrine into a tool of self-salvation. Faith as the state of being grasped by an ultimate was distorted and became the belief in doctrine. Thus faith as the reception of the message that one is accepted became a proposition for intellectual affirmation. But the demand for such an affirmation cannot help raising further questions. Do I really believe? Is not my belief a transitory suppression of doubt and of cognitive honesty? And, if I do not really believe, is my salvation lost? The terrible inner struggles between the will to be honest and the will to be saved show the failure of doctrinal self-salvation.

In contrast to both the sacramental and the doctrinal forms of self-salvation, as we have indicated, stands the emotional. For example, pietism demanded radical personal commitment in terms of a conversion experience and a devotional dedication of one's life (including legal and doctrinal elements of self-surrender). The temptation to self-salvation is present in pietism and in revivalism of all forms, for they provoke the desire for emotions which are not genuine but are artificially created. This happens through evangelists and through artificially

directing one's own emotional possibilities toward conversion and sanctification experiences. In that situation elements of self-salvation are
brought into the orbit of the divine acts of salvation which one wishes
to appropriate.

The personal encounter with God and the reunion with him are the
heart of all genuine religion. It presupposes the presence of a transforming power and the turn toward the ultimate from all preliminary
concerns. Yet, in its distorted form, "piety" becomes a tool with which
to achieve a transformation within one's self. But anything which is imposed upon man's spiritual life by himself or by others remains artificial,
producing anxiety, fanaticism, and the intensification of works of piety.
It discloses the final failure of the pietistic way of self-salvation.

All ways of self-salvation distort the way of salvation. The general
rule that the negative lives from the distortion of the positive is also
valid in this case. This shows the inadequacy of a theology which identifies religion with the human attempt at self-salvation and derives both
from man in his state of estrangement. Actually, even the awareness of
estrangement and the desire for salvation are effects of the presence of
saving power, in other words, revelatory experiences. The same is true
of the ways of self-salvation. Legalism presupposes the reception of the
law in a revelatory experience; asceticism, the awareness of the infinite
as judging the finite; mysticism, the experience of ultimacy in being
and meaning; sacramental self-salvation, the gift of the sacramental
presence; doctrinal self-salvation, the gift of manifest truth; emotional
self-salvation, the transforming power of the holy. Without these presuppositions, man's attempts at self-salvation could not even begin.
Falsa religio is not identical with special historical religions but with
the self-saving attempts in every religion, even in Christianity.

3. Non-historical and Historical Expectations of the New Being

The quest for the New Being is universal because the human predicament and its ambiguous conquest are universal. It appears in all religions. Even in the few cases in which a completely autonomous culture has developed—as in Greece, Rome, and the modern period of
the Western world—utopian expectation of a new reality is present.
The religious substance is effective under the secular form. The character of the quest for the New Being changes from religion to religion

and from culture to culture. However, one can distinguish two main types in polar relation, that is, partly conflicting with each other and partly in unity. The decisive difference refers to the role of history in both types: the New Being can be sought above history, and it can be understood as the aim of history. The first type is predominantly non-historical; the second type, predominantly historical.

For instance, most polytheistic religions are predominantly non-historical. The mystical reactions against polytheism found in Brahmanism and Buddhism and the humanistic reactions against polytheism in classical Greece are, however, also non-historical. In these, as in other expressions of ultimate concern, the New Being is divine power, appearing in many ways to overcome the human predicament, within the limits of finitude. Here the divine is equally near to and equally remote from each period of history. Certainly, salvation begins in history, because man lives in history. But salvation does not occur through history. If there is a vision of history at all, it is envisaged as a circular, self-repeating movement. Nothing new is created by it. The New Being is not the aim of history but appears in the epiphanies of the gods, in spiritual effects produced by ascetics and seers, in divine incarnations, in oracles, and in spiritual elevation. Such divine manifestations are received by individuals; they can be communicated to disciples, but they are not directed to groups. A group, whether a family or mankind as a whole, does not participate in the effects of the New Being. The misery of mankind in history is not to be changed, but individuals may transcend the whole sphere of existence—things, men, and gods. The New Being in this interpretation is the negation of all beings and the affirmation of the Ground of Being alone. One could say that the price paid for the New Being is the negation of everything that has being. This is the root of the difference in the East and West in the feeling for life.

In the West, religion and culture have been determined by the historical type, by the expectation of the New Being in the historical process. This belief is found in ancient Persia, Judaism, Christianity, Islam, and also in a secularized form in some strains of modern humanism. The New Being is expected predominantly in a horizontal direction rather than from the vertical one. The whole of reality is affirmed because it is considered to be essentially good. Its essential goodness is not vitiated by its existential estrangement. But the expectation of the

New Being is the expectation of a transformed reality. The transformation occurs in and through a historical process which is unique, unrepeatable, irreversible. Bearers of this process are historical groups, such as families, nations, and the church; individuals bear it only in relation to historical groups. The actualization of the New Being occurs differently according to the forms of the historical type. It occurs either in a slow progress, in definite qualitative degrees, in the center of the whole process, or at its end when history is elevated to eternity. Some of the possibilities are frequently combined (this is not the place to discuss them systematically). But it can be stated that in Christianity the decisive event occurs in the center of history and that it is precisely the event that gives history a center; that Christianity is also aware of the "not-yet," which is the main emphasis in Judaism; and that Christianity knows the revelatory possibilities in every moment of history. All this is included in the title of the "Christ," the name which Christianity applied to the bearer of the New Being in its final manifestation.

4. THE SYMBOL OF "CHRIST," ITS HISTORICAL AND ITS TRANSHISTORICAL MEANING

The history of the symbol "Messiah" ("Christ") shows that its origin transcends both Christianity and Judaism, thus confirming the universal human expectation of a new reality. When Christianity used this symbol for what it believed to be the central event in history, it accepted—as the religion of the Old Testament had done before it—a large amount of symbolic material taken from the social organization of the Semitic and Egyptian world, especially from the political institution of kingship. The Messiah, the "anointed one," is the king. He conquers the enemies and establishes peace and justice. The more the political meaning of the idea was transcended, the more symbolic the figure of the king became. More and more mythological traits were affixed to it. But the Messiah always remained related to history, i.e., to a historical group, its past and its future. The Messiah does not save individuals in a path leading out of historical existence; he is to transform historical existence. The individual enters a new reality which embraces society and nature. In messianic thought, the New Being does not demand the sacrifice of finite being; instead, it fulfils all finite being by conquering its estrangement.

The strictly historical character of the messianic idea made it possible to transfer the messianic function to a nation, a small group in a nation (the remnant), a social class (proletariat), etc. And it was possible to amalgamate the messianic figure with others, such as the "Servant of Jahweh," the "Son of Man," or the "Man from Above." Something even more important was possible: namely, that the historical type of the expectation of the New Being could include the non-historical type. In this respect Christianity could claim to be the universal type. The universal quest for the New Being is a consequence of universal revelation. If it claims universality, Christianity implicitly maintains that the different forms in which the quest for the New Being has been màde are fulfilled in Jesus as the Christ. Christianity must show—and has always tried to show—that the historical type of the expectation of the New Being embraces itself and the non-historical type, while the non-historical is unable to embrace the historical type. Christianity, in order to be universally valid, must unite the horizontal direction of the expectation of the New Being with the vertical one. For this task Christian theology was provided with conceptual tools by late Judaism. In the period after the Exile, Jewish piety created symbols which combined historical and transhistorical elements and which could be applied to the event of "Jesus" in a universal way. In apocalyptic literature the Messiah is elevated to cosmic significance, the law is declared to have eternal reality, and the divine Wisdom, standing beside God, is a principle of creation and salvation. Other divine qualities have a kind of ontological independence under Jahweh. The figure of the Son of Man combines transcendent roots with historical functions. On this basis the Fourth Gospel strongly emphasized the vertical line in the Logos doctrine, in its stress upon the transhistorical character of Jesus and in its teaching of the presence of judgment and salvation in him. The receding of the eschatological consciousness of early Christianity led to an almost exclusive emphasis on individual salvation. This is already visible in Paul, whose Christ-mysticism and doctrine of the Spirit provided an important bridge across which the non-historical type could enter Christianity. Under these circumstances it is not astonishing that the horizontal line, derived from the Old Testament, was in danger of annihilation by the vertical line, derived from Hellenism. In the Gnostic mixture of religious motifs the danger became reality. The two interdependent symbols of creation and consummation were obliterated. In this situation Christianity was forced into a life-and-death struggle to preserve the Old Testament within the church, the historical type of the expectation of the New Being. The church made this decision and saved the historical character of Christianity. This must be defended in all periods, but in such a way that the universal significance of Christianity is not lost and replaced by the conditioned validity of a contingent historical movement.

5. The Meaning of Paradox in Christian Theology

The Christian assertion that the New Being has appeared in Jesus as the Christ is paradoxical. It constitutes the only all-embracing paradox of Christianity. Whenever the words "paradox" and "paradoxical" are used, a semantic investigation is necessary. These words are abused to such a degree that their application to the Christian event produces confusion and resentment. The paradoxical must be distinguished from the following: the reflective-rational, the dialectical-rational, the irrational, the absurd, and the nonsensical.

The reflective-rational can also be called the realm of technical reason, namely, the kind of thinking which not only follows the laws of formal logic (as all thinking must) but also believes that the only dimensions of being are those which can be totally grasped with the tool of formal logic. If "paradoxical" is understood as the destruction of formal logic, it obviously must be rejected; for even the destruction of formal logic demands the use of formal logic. It cannot be destroyed, but it must be limited to its legal use. The paradox is no exemption to such legal use. In order to place it rightly, one needs formal logic.

The paradoxical has often been confused with the dialectical. Dialectical thinking is rational, not paradoxical. Dialectic is not reflective, in so far as it does not reflect like a mirror the realities with which it deals. It does not look at them merely from the outside. It enters them, so to speak, and participates in their inner tensions. The tensions may appear first in contrasting concepts, but they must be followed down to their roots in the deeper levels of reality. In a dialectical description one element of a concept drives to another. Taken in this sense, dialectics determine all life-processes and must be applied in biology, psychology, and sociology. The description of tensions in living organisms, neurotic conflicts, and class struggles is dialectical. Life itself is dialectical. If applied symbolically to the divine life, God as a living God must be described in dialectical statements. He has the character of all life, namely, to go beyond himself and to return to himself. This is expressed in the Trinitarian symbols. It must be stated with great emphasis that Trinitarian thinking is dialectical and in this sense rational, not paradoxical. This implies a relation in God between the infinite and the finite. God is infinite, in so far as he is the creative ground of the finite and eternally produces the finite potentialities in himself. The finite does not limit him but belongs to the eternal process of his life. All this is dialectical and rational in character; yet in every statement it points to the divine mystery. In all its expressions theology refers to the divine mystery—the mystery of eternal being. The tools of theology are rational, dialectical, and paradoxical; they are not mysterious in speaking of the divine mystery.

The theological paradox is not "irrational." But the transition from essence to existence, from the potential to the actual, from dreaming innocence to existential guilt and tragedy, is irrational. In spite of its universality, this transition is not rational; in the last analysis it is irrational. We encounter the irrationality of this transition from essence to existence in everything, and its presence is irrational, not paradoxical. It is an undeniable fact which must be accepted, although it contradicts the essential structure of everything created.

It would be unnecessary to confront the paradoxical with the absurd if it were not for the confusing phrase, *credo quia absurdum,* which has been wrongly attributed to Tertullian, and if it were not for the fact that the paradoxical has been identified with the absurd. Combinations of logically compatible words become absurd when they contradict the meaningful order of reality. Therefore, the absurd lies in the neighborhood of the grotesque and the ridiculous. We have used this term several times in rejecting symbolic literalism and its grotesque consequences. Such absurdities, however, have no relation to the paradox of the Christian message.

Finally, the paradox is not nonsense. It should be unnecessary to state this, but it is not. Unfortunately, there are always theologians who indulge in the production of propositions which have no meaning semantically and who, in the name of the Christian faith, insist that one has to accept them in order to be a true Christian. They argue that divine truth is above human reason. But the divine truth cannot be expressed in meaningless propositions. Everybody could formulate sentences of this type indefinitely, but they would not make sense; and the paradox is not nonsense.

We have already touched on the relation of the divine mystery to the different logical categories which were compared with paradox. Mystery does not belong in this series. It is present whenever one speaks of God and divine "things." It is based on the nature of the divine itself, its infinity and eternity, its unconditional and ultimate character, its transcendence of the subject-object structure of reality. This mystery of the divine is the presupposition of all theology. But it does not exclude the *logos* of *theos* and, with it, theology as such. The *logos* of *theos* must be expressed in reflective, dialetical, and paradoxical terms. But *theos,* the divine mystery, transcends all of them. Those who pile paradox upon paradox are not nearer to the divine mystery than those who, with the tools of reflective reason, give an account of the semantic meaning of religious concepts—supposing that both acknowledge the ultimate mystery of being.

After this limited discussion of the concept of the paradoxical, we must state in affirmative terms that the concept should be understood in the literal sense of the word. That is paradoxical which contradicts the *doxa,* the opinion which is based on the whole of ordinary human experience, including the empirical and the rational. The Christian paradox contradicts the opinion derived from man's existential predicament and all expectations imaginable on the basis of this predicament. The "offense" given by the paradoxical character of the Christian message is not against the laws of understandable speech but against man's ordinary interpretation of his predicament with respect to himself, his world, and the ultimate underlying both of them. It is an offense against man's unshaken reliance upon himself, his self-saving attempts, and his resignation to despair. Against each of these three attitudes the manifestation of the New Being in Christ is judgment and promise. The appearance of the New Being under the conditions of existence, yet judging and conquering them, is the paradox of the Christian message. This is the only paradox and the source of all paradoxical statements in Christianity. The paradoxical statement that the situation of the Christian is *simul peccator, simul justus* ("at the same time unjust and just," namely, justified) is not a paradox beside the christological paradox: that Jesus is the Christ. Historically and systematically, everything else in Christianity is a corroboration of the simple assertion that Jesus is the Christ. This is neither irrational nor absurd, and it is neither reflectively nor dialectically rational; but it is paradoxical, that is, against man's self-understanding and expectations. The paradox is a new reality and not a logical riddle.

6. God, Man, and the Symbol of the "Christ"

The right understanding of the paradox is essential for considering the meaning of "Christ" as the bearer of the New Being in his relation to God, man, and the universe. Obviously, answers to such considerations are not a matter of detached observation of pre-Christian ideas concerning the Messiah; they are the result of an existential interpretation of both pre-Christian ideas and their criticism and fulfilment in Jesus as the Christ. This corresponds to the method of correlation, in which questions and answers determine each other, and the question about the manifestation of the New Being is asked both on the basis of the human predicament and in the light of the answer which is accepted as *the* answer of Christianity.

The first concept often used for the Christ is "the Mediator." Mediator gods appear in the history of religion at the moment in which the highest God becomes increasingly abstract and removed. They appear in paganism as well as in Judaism and give expression to man's desire to experience his ultimate concern in a concrete manifestation. In paganism the mediator-gods can become gods in their own right; in Judaism they are subjected to Jahweh. "Mediating" in Christianity means bridging the infinite gap between the infinite and the finite, between the unconditional and the conditioned. But the function of mediating is more than merely making the ultimate concrete. Mediation is reunion. The mediator has a saving function; he is the savior. Of course, he is the savior not on his own account but by divine destiny, so that salvation and mediation really come from God. The savior does not save God from the necessity of condemning. Every mediating and saving activity comes from God. God is the subject, not the object, of mediation and salvation. He does not need to be reconciled to man, but he asks man to be reconciled to him.

Therefore, if the Christ is expected as mediator and savior, he is not expected as a third reality between God and man, but as him who represents God to man. He does not represent man to God but shows what God wants man to be. He represents to those who live under the conditions of existence what man essentially is and therefore ought to be under these conditions. It is inadequate and a source of a false Christology to say that the mediator is an ontological reality beside God and man. This could only be a half-god who at the same time is half-man. Such a third being could neither represent God to men nor man to men. It is essential man who represents not only man to man but God to man; for essential man, by his very nature, represents God. He represents the original image of God embodied in man, but he does so under the conditions of estrangement between God and man. The paradox of the Christian message is not that essential humanity includes the union of God and man. This belongs to the dialectics of the infinite and the finite. The paradox of the Christian message is that in *one* personal life essential manhood has appeared under the conditions of existence without being conquered by them. One could also speak of essential God-manhood in order to indicate the divine presence in essential manhood; but this is redundant, and the clarity of thought is served best in speaking simply of essential manhood.

The second concept which needs revision in the light of our understanding of the Christian paradox is that of "Incarnation." The fact that it is not a biblical term is a possible argument against its use as a religious term, though it is not an argument against its theological use. As a theological interpretation of the event on which Christianity is based, it needs careful theological scrutiny and sharp delineation. The first question to consider is obviously: Who is the subject of Incarnation? If the answer is "God," one often continues by saying that "God has become man" and that this is the paradox of the Christian message. But the assertion that "God has become man" is not a paradoxical but a nonsensical statement. It is a combination of words which makes sense only if it is not meant to mean what the words say. The word "God" points to ultimate reality, and even the most consistent Scotists had to admit that the only thing God cannot do is to cease to be God. But that is just what the assertion that "God has become man" means. Even if one speaks of God as "becoming," he still remains God in each moment. He does not become something that is not God. Therefore, it is preferable to speak of a divine being which has become man and to refer to the terms "Son of God" or the "Spiritual Man" or the "Man from Above," as they are used in biblical language. Any one of these designations so used is not nonsensical but is dangerous for two reasons: first, there is the polytheistic connotation of divine beings besides God, and, second, incarnation is interpreted in terms of a mythology in which divine beings are transmuted into natural objects or human beings. In this sense incarnation is far from being a characteristic of Christianity. It is, on the contrary, a characteristic of paganism in so far as, within it, no god has overcome the finite basis on which he stands. Because of this, the mythological imagination within polytheism has had no difficulty in transforming divine beings into both natural objects and human beings. The unqualified use of the term "Incarnation" in Christianity creates pagan, or at least superstitious, connotations.

A modifying interpretation of the term "Incarnation" would have to follow the Johannine statement that the "Logos became flesh." "Logos" is the principle of the divine self-manifestation in God as well as in the universe, in nature as well as in history. "Flesh" does not mean a material substance but stands for historical existence. And "became" points to the paradox of God participating in that which did not receive him and in that which is estranged from him. This is not a myth of transmutation but the assertion that God is manifest in a personal life-process as a saving participant in the human predicament. If "Incarnation" is understood in this qualifying way, then the Christian paradox can be expressed by this term. But perhaps this is an unwise course, since it is practically impossible to protect the concept from superstitious connotations.

In discussing the character of the quest for and the expectation of the Christ, a question arises which has been carefully avoided by many traditional theologians, even though it is consciously or unconsciously alive for most contemporary people. It is the problem of how to understand the meaning of the symbol "Christ" in the light of the immensity of the universe, the heliocentric system of planets, the infinitely small part of the universe which man and his history constitute, and the possibility of other "worlds" in which divine self-manifestations may appear and be received. Such developments become especially important if one considers that biblical and related expectations envisaged the coming of the Messiah within a cosmic frame. The universe will be reborn into a new eon. The function of the bearer of the New Being is not only to save individuals and to transform man's historical existence but to renew the universe. And the assumption is that mankind and individual men are so dependent on the powers of the universe that salvation of the one without the other is unthinkable.

The basic answer to these questions is given in the concept of essential man appearing in a personal life under the conditions of existential estrangement. This restricts the expectation of the Christ to historical mankind. The man in whom essential man has appeared in existence represents human history; more precisely, as its central event, he creates the meaning of human history. It is the eternal relation of God to man which is manifest in the Christ. At the same time, our basic answer leaves the universe open for possible divine manifestations in other areas or periods of being. Such possibilities cannot be denied. But they cannot be proved or disproved. Incarnation is unique for the special group in which it happens, but it is not unique in the sense that other singular incarnations for other unique worlds are excluded. Man cannot claim that the infinite has entered the finite to overcome its existential estrangement in mankind alone. Man cannot claim to occupy the only possible place for Incarnation. Although statements about other worlds and God's relation to them cannot be verified experientially, they are important because they help to interpret the meaning of terms like "mediator," "savior," "Incarnation," "the Messiah," and "the new eon."

Perhaps one can go a step further. The interdependence of everything with everything else in the totality of being includes a participation of nature in history and demands a participation of the universe in salvation. Therefore, if there are non-human "worlds" in which existential estrangement is not only real—as it is in the whole universe—but in which there is also a type of awareness of this estrangement, such worlds cannot be without the operation of saving power within them. Otherwise self-destruction would be the inescapable consequence. The manifestation of saving power in one place implies that saving power is operating in all places. The expectation of the Messiah as the bearer of the New Being presupposes that "God loves the universe," even though in the appearance of the Christ he actualizes this love for historical man alone.

In the last sections we have analyzed the expectation of the New Being, the meaning of the symbol "Christ," and the validity of the different concepts in which theology has interpreted this meaning. We have not yet spoken of the actual appearance of the Christ in Jesus, although, according to the theological circle, this is presupposed in the description of the expectation. We now turn to the event which, according to the Christian message, has fulfilled the expectations, namely, the event which is called "Jesus, the Christ."

II

THE REALITY OF THE CHRIST

A. JESUS AS THE CHRIST

1. THE NAME "JESUS CHRIST"

CHRISTIANITY is what it is through the affirmation that Jesus of Nazareth, who has been called "the Christ," is actually the Christ, namely, he who brings the new state of things, the New Being. Wherever the assertion that Jesus is the Christ is maintained, there is the Christian message; wherever this assertion is denied, the Christian message is not affirmed. Christianity was born, not with the birth of the man who is called "Jesus," but in the moment in which one of his followers was driven to say to him, "Thou art the Christ." And Christianity will live as long as there are people who repeat this assertion. For the event on which Christianity is based has two sides: the fact which is called "Jesus of Nazareth" and the reception of this fact by those who received him as the Christ. The first of those who received him as the Christ in the early tradition was named Simon Peter. This event is reported in a story in the center of the Gospel of Mark; it takes place near Caesarea Philippi and marks the turning point in the narrative. The moment of the disciples' acceptance of Jesus as the Christ is also the moment of his rejection by the powers of history. This gives the story its tremendous symbolic power. He who is the Christ has to die for his acceptance of the title "Christ." And those who continue to call him the Christ must assert the paradox that he who is supposed to overcome existential estrangement must participate in it and its self-destructive consequences. This is the central story of the Gospel. Reduced to its simplest form, it is the statement that the man Jesus of Nazareth is the Christ.

The first step demanded of christological thought is an interpretation of the name "Jesus Christ," preferably in the light of the Caesarea Philippi story. One must clearly see that Jesus Christ is not an individual name, consisting of a first and a second name, but that it is the combination of an individual name—the name of a certain man who lived in Nazareth between the years 1 and 30—with the title "the Christ," expressing in the mythological tradition a special figure with a special function. The Messiah—in Greek, *Christos*—is the "anointed one" who has received an unction from God enabling him to establish the reign of God in Israel and in the world. Therefore, the name Jesus Christ must be understood as "Jesus who is called the Christ," or "Jesus who is the Christ," or "Jesus as the Christ," or "Jesus the Christ." The context determines which of these interpretative phrases should be used; but one of them should be used in order to keep the original meaning of the name "Jesus Christ" alive, not only in theological thought but also in ecclesiastical practice. Christian preaching and teaching must continually re-emphasize the paradox that the man Jesus is called the Christ—a paradox which is often drowned in the liturgical and homiletic use of "Jesus Christ" as a proper name. "Jesus Christ" means—originally, essentially, and permanently—"Jesus who is the Christ."

2. EVENT, FACT, AND RECEPTION

Jesus as the Christ is both a historical fact and a subject of believing reception. One cannot speak the truth about the event on which Christianity is based without asserting both sides. Many theological mistakes could have been avoided if these two sides of the "Christian event" had been emphasized with equal strength. And Christian theology as a whole is undercut if one of them is completely ignored. If theology ignores the fact to which the name of Jesus of Nazareth points, it ignores the basic Christian assertion that Essential God-Manhood has appeared within existence and subjected itself to the conditions of existence without being conquered by them. If there were no personal life in which existential estrangement had been overcome, the New Being would have remained a quest and an expectation and would not be a reality in time and space. Only if the existence is conquered in *one* point—a personal life, representing existence as a whole—is it conquered in principle, which means "in beginning and in power." This is the reason that Christian theology must insist on the actual fact to which the name Jesus of Nazareth refers. It is why the church prevailed against competing groups in the religious movements of the first centuries. This is the reason that the church had to fight a vehement struggle with the gnostic-docetic elements within itself—elements which entered Christianity as early as the New Testament. And this is the reason that anyone who takes seriously the historical approach to the New Testament and its critical methods becomes suspect of docetic ideas, however strongly he may emphasize the factual side of the message of Jesus the Christ.

Nevertheless, the other side, the believing reception of Jesus *as* the Christ, calls for equal emphasis. Without this reception the Christ would not have been the Christ, namely, the manifestation of the New Being in time and space. If Jesus had not impressed himself as the Christ on his disciples and through them upon all following generations, the man who is called Jesus of Nazareth would perhaps be remembered as a historically and religiously important person. As such, he would belong to the preliminary revelation, perhaps to the preparatory segment of the history of revelation. He could then have been a prophetic anticipation of the New Being, but not the final manifestation of the New Being itself. He would not have been the Christ even if he had claimed to be the Christ. The receptive side of the Christian event is as important as the factual side. And only their unity creates the event upon which Christianity is based. According to later symbolism, the Christ is the head of the church, which is his body. As such, they are necessarily interdependent.

Church.

3. History and the Christ

If the Christ is not the Christ without those who receive him as the Christ, what would it mean for the validity of this message if the continuity of the church as the group which receives him as the Christ were interrupted or destroyed? It could be imagined—and today more easily than ever—that the historical tradition in which Jesus appears as the center would break down completely. It could be imagined that a total catastrophe and a completely new beginning of the human race would leave no memory of the event "Jesus as the Christ." Can such a possibility—which is neither verifiable nor refutable—undercut the assertion that Jesus is the Christ, or does the Christian faith forbid such speculation? The latter alternative has become impossible for those who realize that today this possibility has become an actual threat! After mankind has gained the power to extinguish itself, this question cannot be repressed. Would the suicide of mankind be a refutation of the Christian message?

Cl.

The New Testament is aware of the problem of historical continuity, and it clearly indicates that so long as there is human history—namely, up to the end of the world—the New Being in Jesus as the Christ is present and effective. Jesus the Christ will be with those who believe in him every day up to the end of time. The "thresholds of hell," the demonic powers, will not conquer his church. And, before the end, he will establish his "reign of a thousand years" and will come as the judge of all beings. How can such assertions be combined with the possibility that mankind may destroy itself tomorrow? And even if human beings were left who were cut off from the historical tradition in which Jesus as the Christ has appeared, one must still ask: "What do the biblical assertions mean in view of such a development?" One cannot answer in terms of ordering God not to allow such catastrophes. For the structure of the universe clearly indicates that the conditions of life on earth are limited in time, and the conditions of human life even more so. If one dismisses a supranaturalistic literalism with respect to the eschatological symbols, one must understand in a different way the relation of Jesus as the Christ to human history.

We have discussed a similar problem in connection with the relation of the idea of the Christ to the universe. The question concerned the significance of the idea of the Christ in terms of spatial extension; the present question concerns the significance of the reality of Jesus as the Christ in terms of temporal extension. We have answered the first question by saying that the relation of Eternal God-Manhood to human existence does not exclude other relations of God to other sections or levels of the existing universe. The Christ is God-for-us! But God is not only for us, he is for everything created. In an analogous way one has to say that Jesus as the Christ is related to that historical development of which he is the center, determining its beginning and its end. It begins the moment human beings start realizing their existential estrangement and raise the question of the New Being. Obviously, such a beginning cannot be determined by historical research but must be told in legendary and mythical terms, as in the Bible and other religious literature. Corresponding to this beginning, the end is the moment in which the continuity of that history in which Jesus as the Christ is the center is definitely broken. This moment cannot be determined empirically, either in its nature or in its causes. Its nature may be the disappearance or a complete transformation of what once was historical mankind. Its causes may be historical, biological, or physical. In any case, it would be the end of that development of which Jesus as the Christ is the center. In faith it is certain that for historical mankind in its unique, continuous development, as experienced here and now, Christ is the center. But faith cannot judge about the future destiny of historical mankind and the way it will come to an end. Jesus is the Christ for us, namely, for those who participate in the historical continuum which he determines in its meaning. This existential limitation does not qualitatively limit his significance, but it leaves open other ways of divine self-manifestations before and after our historical continuum.

4. The Research for the Historical Jesus and Its Failure

From the moment that the scientific method of historical research was applied to biblical literature, theological problems which were never completely absent became intensified in a way unkown to former periods of church history. The historical method unites analytical-critical and constructive-conjectural elements. For the average Christian consciousness shaped by the orthodox doctrine of verbal inspiration, the first element was much more impressive than the second. One felt only the negative element in the term "criticism" and called the whole enterprise "historical criticism" or "higher criticism" or, with reference to a recent method, "form criticism." In itself, the term "historical criticism" means nothing more than historical research. Every historical research criticizes its sources, separating what has more probability from that which has less or is altogether improbable. Nobody doubts the validity of this method, since it is confirmed continuously by its success; and nobody seriously protests if it destroys beautiful legends and deeply rooted prejudices. But biblical research became suspect from its very beginning. It seemed to criticize not only the historical sources but the revelation contained in these sources. Historical research and rejection of biblical authority were identified. Revelation, it was implied, covered not only the revelatory content but also the historical form in which it had appeared. This seemed to be especially true of the facts concerning the "historical Jesus." Since the biblical revelation is essentially historical, it appeared to be impossible to separate the revelatory content from the historical reports as they are given in the biblical records. Historical criticism seemed to undercut faith itself.

But the critical part of historical research into biblical literature is the less important part. More important is the constructive-conjectural part, which was the driving force in the whole enterprise. The facts behind the records, especially the facts about Jesus, were sought. There was an urgent desire to discover the reality of this man, Jesus of Nazareth, behind the coloring and covering traditions which are almost as old as the reality itself. So the research for the so-called "historical Jesus" started. Its motives were religious and scientific at the same time. The attempt was courageous, noble, and extremely significant in many respects. Its theological consequences are numerous and rather important. But, seen in the light of its basic intention, the attempt of historical criticism to find the empirical truth about Jesus of Nazareth was a failure. The historical Jesus, namely, the Jesus behind the symbols of his reception as the Christ, not only did not appear but receded farther and farther with every new step. The history of the attempts to write a "life of Jesus," elaborated by Albert Schweitzer in his early work, *The Quest of the Historical Jesus,* is still valid. His own constructive attempt has been corrected. Scholars, whether conservative or radical, have become more cautious, but the methodological situation has not changed. This became manifest when R. Bultmann's bold program of a "demythologization of the New Testament" aroused a storm in all theological camps and the slumber of Barthianism with respect to the historical problem was followed by an astonished awakening. But the result of the new (and very old) questioning is not a picture of the so-called historical Jesus but the insight that there is no picture behind the biblical one which could be made scientifically probable.

This situation is not a matter of a preliminary shortcoming of historical research which will some day be overcome. It is caused by the nature of the sources itself. The reports about Jesus of Nazareth are those of Jesus as the Christ, given by persons who had received him as the Christ. Therefore, if one tries to find the real Jesus behind the picture of Jesus as the Christ, it is necessary critically to separate the elements which belong to the factual side of the event from the elements which belong to the receiving side. In doing so, one sketches a "Life of Jesus"; and innumerable such sketches have been made. In many of them scientific honesty, loving devotion, and theological interest have worked together. In others critical detachment and even malevolent rejection are visible. But none can claim to be a probable picture which is the result of the tremendous scientific toil dedicated to this task for two hundred years. At best, they are more or less probable results, able to be the basis neither of an acceptance nor of a rejection of the Christian faith.

In view of this situation, there have been attempts to reduce the picture of the historical Jesus to the "essentials," to elaborate a *Gestalt* while leaving the particulars open to doubt. But this is not a way out. Historical research cannot paint an essential picture after all the particular traits have been eliminated because they are questionable. It remains dependent on the particulars. Consequently, the pictures of the historical Jesus in which the form of a "Life of Jesus" is wisely avoided still differ from one another as much as those in which such self-restriction is not applied.

The dependence of the *Gestalt* on the valuation of the particulars is evident in an example taken from the complex of what Jesus thought about himself. In order to elaborate this point, one must know, besides many other things, whether he applied the title "Son of Man" to himself and, if so, in what sense. Every answer given to this question is a more or less probable hypothesis, but the character of the "essential" picture of the historical Jesus depends decisively on this hypothesis. Such an example clearly shows the impossibility of replacing the attempt to portray a "Life of Jesus" by trying to paint the *"Gestalt* of Jesus."

At the same time, this example shows another important point. People who are not familiar with the methodological side of historical research and are afraid of its consequences for Christian doctrine like to attack historical research generally and the research in the biblical literature especially, as being theologically prejudiced. If they are consistent, they will not deny that their own interpretation is also prejudiced or, as they would say, dependent on the truth of their faith. But they deny that the historical method has objective scientific criteria. Such an assertion, however, cannot be maintained in view of the immense historical material which has been discovered and often empirically verified by a universally used method of research. It is characteristic of this method that it tries to maintain a permanent self-criticism in order to liberate itself from any conscious or unconscious prejudice. This is never completely successful, but it is a powerful weapon and necessary for achieving historical knowledge.

One of the examples often given in this context is the treatment of the New Testament miracles. The historical method approaches the miracle stories neither with the assumption that they have happened because they are attributed to him who is called the Christ nor with the assumption that they have not happened because such events would contradict the laws of nature. The historical method asks how trustworthy the records are in every particular case, how dependent they are on older sources, how much they might be influenced by the credulity of a period, how well confirmed they are by other independent sources, in what style they are written, and for what purpose they are used in the whole context. All these questions can be answered in an "objective" way without necessary interference of negative or positive prejudices. The historian never can reach certainty in this way, but he can reach high degrees of probability. It would, however, be a leap to another level if he transformed historical probability into positive or negative historical certainty by a judgment of faith (as will be shown at a later point). This clear distinction is often confused by the obvious fact that the understanding of the meaning of a text is partly dependent on the categories of understanding used in the encounter with texts and records. But it is not wholly dependent on them, since there are philological as well as other aspects which are open to an objective approach. Understanding demands one's participation in what one understands, and we can participate only in terms of what we are, including our own categories of understanding. But this "existential" understanding should never prejudice the judgment of the historian concerning facts and relations. The person whose ultimate concern is the content of the biblical message is in the same position as the one who is indifferent to it if such questions are discussed as the development of the Synoptic tradition, or the mythological and legendary elements of the New Testament. Both have the same criteria of historical probability and must use them with the same rigor, although doing so may affect their own religious or philosophical convictions or prejudices. In this process, it may happen that prejudices which close the eyes to particular facts open them to others. But this "opening of the eyes" is a personal experience which cannot be made into a methodological principle. There is only one methodological procedure, and that is to look at the subject matter and not at one's own looking at the subject matter. Actually, such looking is determined by many psychological, sociological, and historical factors. These aspects must be neglected intentionally by everyone who approaches a fact objectively. One must not formulate a judgment about the self-consciousness of Jesus from the fact that one is a Christian—or an anti-Christian. It must be derived from a degree of plausibility based on records and their probable historical validity. This, of course, presupposes that the content of the Christian faith is independent of this judgment.

The search for the historical Jesus was an attempt to discover a minimum of reliable facts about the man Jesus of Nazareth, in order to provide a safe foundation for the Christian faith. This attempt was a failure. Historical research provided probabilities about Jesus of a higher or lower degree. On the basis of these probabilities, it sketched "Lives of Jesus." But they were more like novels than biographies; they certainly could not provide a safe foundation for the Christian faith. Christianity is not based on the acceptance of a historical novel; it is based on the witness to the messianic character of Jesus by people who were not interested at all in a biography of the Messiah.

The insight into this situation induced some theologians to give up any attempt to construct a "life" or a *Gestalt* of the historical Jesus and to restrict themselves to an interpretation of the "words of Jesus." Most of these words (though not all of them) do not refer to himself and can be separated from any biographical context. Therefore, their meaning is independent of the fact that he may or may not have said them. On that basis the insoluble biographical problem has no bearing on the truth of the words rightly or wrongly recorded as the words of Jesus. That most of the words of Jesus have parallels in contemporaneous Jewish literature is not an argument against their validity. This is not even an argument against their uniqueness and power as they appear in collections like the Sermon on the Mount, the parables, and the discussions with foes and followers alike.[1]

A theology which tries to make the words of Jesus into the historical foundation of the Christian faith can do so in two ways. It can treat the words of Jesus as the "teachings of Jesus" or as the "message of Jesus." As the teachings of Jesus, they are understood as refined interpretations of the natural law or as original insights into the nature of man. They have no relation to the concrete situation in which they are spoken. As such, they belong to the law, prophecy, or Wisdom litera-

[1] This refers also to the discovery of the Dead Sea Scrolls, which—in spite of much sensationalism in the publicity given to it—has opened the eyes of many people to the problem of biblical research but which has not changed the theological situation at all.

ture such as is found in the Old Testament. They may transcend all three categories in terms of depth and power; but they do not transcend them in terms of character. The retreat in historical research to the "teachings of Jesus" reduces Jesus to the level of the Old Testament and implicitly denies his claim to have overcome the Old Testament context.

The second way in which historical research restricts itself to the words of Jesus is more profound than the first. It denies that the words of Jesus are general rules of human behavior, that they are rules to which one has to subject one's self, or that they are universal and can therefore be abstracted from the situation in which they were spoken. Instead, they emphasize Jesus' message that the Kingdom of God is "at hand" and that those who want to enter it must decide for or against the Kingdom of God. These words of Jesus are not general rules but concrete demands. This interpretation of the historical Jesus, suggested especially by Rudolf Bultmann, identifies the meaning of Jesus with that of his message. He calls for a decision, namely, the decision for God. And this decision includes the acceptance of the Cross, by his own acceptance of the Cross. The historically impossible, namely, to sketch a "life" or a *Gestalt* of Jesus, is ingeniously avoided by using the immediately given—namely, his message about the Kingdom of God and its conditions—and by keeping as nearly as possible to the "paradox of the Cross of the Christ." But even this method of restricted historical judgment cannot give a foundation to the Christian faith. It does not show how the requirement of deciding for the Kingdom of God can be fulfilled. The situation of having to decide remains one of being under the law. It does not transcend the Old Testament situation, the situation of the quest for the Christ. One could call this theology "existentialist liberalism" in contrast to the "legalist liberalism" of the first. But neither method can answer the question of wherein lies the power to obey the teachings of Jesus or to make the decision for the Kingdom of God. This these methods cannot do because the answer must come from a new reality, which, according to the Christian message, is the New Being in Jesus as the Christ. The Cross is the symbol of a gift before it is the symbol of a demand. But, if this is accepted, it is impossible to retreat from the being of the Christ to his words. The last avenue of the search for the historical Jesus is barred, and the failure of the attempt to give a foundation to the Christian faith through historical research becomes obvious.

This result would probably have been more easily acknowledged if it had not been for the semantic confusion about the meaning of the term "historical Jesus." The term was predominantly used for the results of historical research into the character and life of the person who stands behind the Gospel reports. Like all historical knowledge, our knowledge of this person is fragmentary and hypothetical. Historical research subjects this knowledge to methodological skepticism and to continuous change in particulars as well as essentials. Its ideal is to reach a high degree of probability, but in many cases this is impossible.

The term "historical Jesus" is also used to mean that the event "Jesus as the Christ" has a factual element. The term in this sense raises the question of faith and not the question of historical research. If the factual element in the Christian event were denied, the foundation of Christianity would be denied. Methodological skepticism about the work of historical research does not deny this element. Faith cannot even guarantee the name "Jesus" in respect to him who was the Christ. It must leave that to the incertitudes of our historical knowledge. But faith does guarantee the factual transformation of reality in that personal life which the New Testament expresses in its picture of Jesus as the Christ. No fruitful and honest discussion is possible if these two meanings of the term "historical Jesus" are not clearly distinguished.

5. HISTORICAL RESEARCH AND THEOLOGY

If the attempt to give a foundation to Christian faith and theology through historical research is a failure, the question arises as to whether historical research has other functions in Christianity. It certainly has. The historical approach to biblical literature is one of the great events in the history of Christianity and even of religion and human culture. It is one of the elements of which Protestantism can be proud. It was an expression of Protestant courage when theologians subjected the holy writings of their own church to a critical analysis through the historical method. It appears that no other religion in human history exercised such boldness and took upon itself the same risk. Certainly Islam, orthodox Judaism, and Roman Catholicism did not do so. This courage received its reward, in that Protestantism was able to join the general historical consciousness and was not forced into an isolated and narrow spiritual world without influence in the creative development of spiritual life. Protestantism (except in its fundamentalistic groups) was not driven into that unconscious dishonesty wherein the results of historical research are rejected on the basis of dogmatic prejudice, not on the basis of evidence. This was a daring attitude and not without serious risk. But the Protestant groups which took this risk have kept alive, in spite of the various crises into which radical historical criticism threw them. It became more and more manifest that the Christian assertion that Jesus is the Christ does not contradict the most uncompromising historical honesty. Of course, the way in which this assertion is expressed has had to be changed under the impact of the historical approach.

The first and most important of these changes is that theology has learned to distinguish between the empirically historical, the legendary, and the mythological elements in the biblical stories of both Testaments. It discovered criteria for these different forms of semantic expression and applied them with the methodological strictness employed by every good historian. It is obvious that this distinction between three semantic forms has important consequences for the work of the systematic theologian. It prevents him from giving dogmatic validity to judgments which belong to the realm of higher or lower probability. If he makes historical decisions, he can do so only as a historian, not as an interpreter of the Christian faith. He cannot give dogmatic validity to historically probable judgments. Whatever faith can do in its own dimension, it cannot overrule historical judgments. It cannot make the historically improbable probable, or the probable improbable, or the probable or improbable certain. The certitude of faith does not imply certainty about questions of historical research. This insight is widespread today and is the greatest contribution of historical research to systematic theology. But it is not the only one; there are several others, one being the insight into the development of the christological symbols.

By analyzing the difference between historical, legendary, and mythical elements in the Gospel reports, historical research has given systematic theology a tool for dealing with the christological symbols of the Bible. Systematic theology cannot escape this task, since it is through these symbols that theology from the very beginning has tried to give the "logos" of the Christian message in order to show its rationality. Some christological symbols used in the New Testament are: Son of David, Son of Man, Heavenly Man, Messiah, Son of God, Kyrios, Logos. There are still others of less significance. They develop in the following four steps: The first to be mentioned is that these symbols have arisen and grown in their own religious culture and language. The second is the use of these symbols by those to whom they had become alive as expressions of their self-interpretation and as answers to the questions implied in their existential predicament. The third is the transformation that these symbols underwent in meaning when used to interpret the event on which Christianity is based. The fourth is their distortion by popular superstition, supported by theological literalism and supranaturalism. Examples of these four steps in the development of the christological symbols will disclose the validity of this analysis.

The symbol "Son of Man," which is used most frequently by Jesus in pointing to himself in all Four Gospels, designates an original unity between God and man. Especially is this the case if one accepts a connection between the Persian symbol of the Original Man and the Paulinian idea of the Spiritual Man. This is the first step delineated above or applied to the symbol "Son of Man." The second one follows from the way in which the Man from Above is contrasted with man's situation of existential estrangement from God, his world, and himself. This contrast includes the expectation that the Son of Man will conquer the forces of estrangement and re-establish the unity between God and man. In the third step the symbol "Son of Man" (or one of the corroborating symbols) is recorded as Jesus applying the term to himself, as, for instance, in the trial scene before the High Priest. The original vision of the function of the Son of Man is decisively transformed in this account. This is so much the case that the accusation of blasphemy for calling himself the Son of Man who will appear as the judge of this eon on the clouds of the sky was understandable. Literalism takes the fourth step by imagining a transcendent being who, once upon a time, was sent down from his heavenly place and transmuted into a man. In this way a true and powerful symbol becomes an absurd story, and the Christ becomes a half-god, a particular being between God and man.

The symbol "Son of God," applied to the Christ, can be dealt with in the same four steps. In biblical language, "sonship" means an intimate relationship between father and son. Man in his essential nature, in his "dreaming innocence," has such a relation to God. Israel has gained it by her election to sonship. In paganism certain divine or half-divine figures are sons of a god. Although these two ways of using the symbol "Son of God" differ greatly, they have the presupposition in common that human nature makes possible a father-son relation between God and man. But this relation has been lost by man's estrangement from God, by his self-elevation against God, and by his turning away from God. Sonship to God has ceased to be a universal fact. Only special divine acts can re-establish it. Christianity considers the Christ as the "only begotten son of God," thus putting him in contrast to all other men and their natural, although lost, sonship to God. "Son of God" becomes the title of the one in whom the essential unity of God and man has appeared under the conditions of existence. The essentially universal becomes existentially unique. But this uniqueness is not exclusive. Everyone who participates in the New Being actualized in him receives the power of becoming a child of God himself. The son re-establishes the child character of every man in relation to God, a character which is essentially human. This use of the "Son of God" symbol transcends the Jewish as well as the pagan use. Being the Son of God means representing the essential unity between God and man under the conditions of existence and re-establishing this unity in all those who participate in his being. The symbol becomes distorted if it is taken literally and a human family situation is projected into the inner life of the divine. Literalists often ask whether one believes that "Jesus was the Son of God." Those who ask this question think that they know what the term "Son of God" means and that the only problem is whether this known designation can be attributed to the man Jesus of Nazareth. If the question is asked in this way, it cannot be answered, because either an affirmative or a negative answer would be wrong. The only way to answer the question is to ask another one, namely, What do you mean if you use the term "Son of God"? If one receives a literalistic answer to this question, one must reject it as superstitious. If one receives an answer which affirms the symbolic character of the term "Son of God," the meaning of this symbol can then be discussed. Much harm has been done in Christianity by a literalistic understanding of the symbol "Son of God."

We have already dealt with the symbol of "Messiah" or "Christ." But we must reinterpret the symbol in the light of the four steps we have outlined in relation to all christological symbols. The first step points to the historical-transhistorical figure through whom Jahweh will establish his kingdom in Israel and, through Israel, in the whole world. The oscillation between inner-historical and suprahistorical qualities of the Messiah and his kingdom belongs to the essence of the symbol, but in such a way that in the prophetic period the historical emphasis prevailed and in the apocalyptic period the transhistorical element became decisive. The second step is the experience of man's predicament—and the predicament of his world—in actual existence. The actual kingdoms are full of injustice and misery. They stand under demonic rule. This side of the messianic idea was increasingly emphasized in the later period of Judaism and found a very strong expression in the apocalyptic literature. The present eon in its totality, including individuals, society, and nature, is perverted. A new eon, a new state of things in the universe, must be asked for. It is the Messiah who will bring it with divine power. These motifs are not restricted to Judaism. They have roots in Persia and resound everywhere in the ancient world. The third step is the reception and transformation of this set of symbols by Christianity: the Messiah who is supposed to bring the new eon is defeated by the powers of the old eon. The defeat of the Messiah on the Cross is the most radical transformation of the symbol of the Messiah, so radical that Judaism up to the present day denies the messianic character of Jesus just for this reason. A defeated Messiah is not a Messiah at all. Christianity acknowledges the paradox—and accepts it. The fourth step is the literalistic distortion of the messianic paradox. It starts with the way in which the title "the Christ" became a part of a proper name and ceased to be the symbolic designation of a function. "Christ" became an individual with supranatural powers who, through a voluntary sacrifice, made it possible for God to save those who believe in him. The paradox of the transformed messianic symbol disappeared.

The last example for the development of the christological symbols is that conceptual symbol which became the main tool for the christological work of the church, "the Logos." It can be called a conceptual symbol because the Logos, as conceived by Stoicism, unites cosmological and religious elements. It unites rational structure and creative power. In Philo and the Fourth Gospel the religious and symbolic quality of the idea of the Logos prevails. But the rational side does not disappear. The rational structure of the universe is mediated through the Logos. This is the first step in the consideration of the symbol of the Logos. In the second the existential background of this idea must be considered. The answer is given by Heraclitus (the creator of the Logos doctrine) when he contrasts the universal logos and its laws with the foolishness of the people and the disorder in society. Stoicism took over this motif and pointed to the unbridgeable gap between the wise one who participates in the Logos and the mass of fools who are separated from, but try to come nearer to, the Logos. In Philo the motif is the unapproachable mystery of God which demands a mediating principle between God and man and drives him to his Logos doctrine. In Christianity—following the Fourth Gospel—both motifs are present. The Logos reveals the mystery and reunites the estranged by appearing as a historical reality in a personal life. And this is the third step in our consideration. The conceptual symbol of the Logos is received and transformed by Christianity. The universal principle of divine self-manifestation is, in its essential character, qualitatively present in an individual human being. He subjects himself to the conditions of existence and conquers existential estrangement within estranged existence. Participation in the universal Logos is dependent on participation in the Logos actualized in a historical personality. Christianity replaces the wise man of Stoicism with the Spiritual man. The Spiritual man is aware of his foolishness as overcome by the foolishness of the Cross, the paradox of him in whom the Logos was present without restriction. Here also a fourth step must be considered, the *re*-mythologization of the conceptual symbol "Logos" into the story of the metamorphosis of a divine being into the man Jesus of Nazareth. The term "Incarnation" is often misunderstood in this way, and some pictorial or artistic expressions of Trinitarian symbolism support such remythologization by identifying the universal principle of the divine self-manifestation with the historical figure of Jesus of Nazareth. Traditional theology protested against this mythologizing by rejecting the absurd idea that the Logos element was lacking in divine life when the Logos was in history. Against such absurdities a demythologization of the symbol of the Logos has been and must be exercised.

Historical criticism is largely responsible for our understanding of the development of christological symbols. They can be used again by theology, for they are liberated from literalistic connotations which made them useless for theology and an unnecessary stumbling block for those who wanted to understand the meaning of the Christian symbols.

This is one of the great indirect contributions of scientific research to theology and faith. Neither faith nor theology is based on these insights, but both are protected by them against superstition and absurdity.

6. FAITH AND HISTORICAL SKEPTICISM

The preceding evaluation of the historical approach to the biblical records led to a negative and a positive assertion. The negative assertion is that historical research can neither give nor take away the foundation of the Christian faith. The positive assertion is that historical research has influenced and must influence Christian theology, first, by giving an analysis of the three different semantic levels of biblical literature (and, analogously, of Christian preaching in all periods); second, by showing in several steps the development of the christological symbols (as well as the other systematically important symbols); and, finally, by providing a precise philological and historical understanding of the biblical literature by means of the best methods developed in all historical work.

But it is necessary systematically to raise once more a question which is continuously being asked with considerable religious anxiety. Does not the acceptance of the historical method for dealing with the source documents of the Christian faith introduce a dangerous insecurity into the thought and life of the church and of every individual Christian? Could not historical research lead to a complete skepticism about the biblical records? Is it not imaginable that historical criticism could come to the judgment that the man Jesus of Nazareth never lived? Did not some scholars, though only a few and not very important ones, make just this statement? And even if such a statement can never be made with certainty, is it not destructive for the Christian faith if the non-existence of Jesus can somehow be made probable, no matter how low the degree of probability? In reply, let us first reject some insufficient and misleading answers. It is inadequate to point out that historical research has not yet given any evidence to support such skepticism. Certainly, it has not yet! But the anxious question remains of whether it could not do so sometime in the future! Faith cannot rest on such unsure ground. The answer, taken from the "not-yet" of skeptical evidence, is insufficient. There is another possible answer, which, though not false, is misleading. This is to say that the historical foundation of Christianity is an essential element of the Christian faith itself and that this faith, through its own power, can overrule skeptical possibilities within historical criticism. It can, it is maintained, guarantee the existence of Jesus of Nazareth and at least the essentials in the biblical picture. But we must analyze this answer carefully, for it is ambiguous. The problem is: Exactly what can faith guarantee? And the inevitable answer is that faith can guarantee only its own foundation, namely, the appearance of that reality which has created the faith. This reality is the New Being, who conquers existential estrangement and thereby makes faith possible. This alone faith is able to guarantee—and that because its own existence is identical with the presence of the New Being. Faith itself is the immediate (not mediated by conclusions) evidence of the New Being within and under the conditions of existence. Precisely that is guaranteed by the very nature of the Christian faith. No historical criticism can question the immediate awareness of those who find themselves transformed into the state of faith. One is reminded of the Augustinian-Cartesian refutation of radical skepticism. That tradition pointed to the immediacy of a self-consciousness which guaranteed itself by its participation in being. By analogy, one must say that participation, not historical argument, guarantees the reality of the event upon which Christianity is based. It guarantees a personal life in which the New Being has conquered the old being. But it does not guarantee his name to be Jesus of Nazareth. Historical doubt concerning the existence and the life of someone with this name cannot be overruled. He might have had another name. (This is a historically absurd, but logically necessary, consequence of the historical method.) Whatever his name, the New Being was and is actual in this man.

But here a very important question arises. How can the New Being who is called "the Christ" transform reality if no concrete trait of his nature is left? Kierkegaard exaggerates when he says that it is sufficient for the Christian faith nakedly to assert that in the years 1–30 God sent his son. Without the concreteness of the New Being, its newness would be empty. Only if existence is conquered concretely and in its manifold aspects, is it actually conquered. The power which has created and preserved the community of the New Being is not an abstract statement about its appearance; it is the picture of him in whom it has appeared. No special trait of this picture can be verified with certainty. But it can be definitely asserted that through this picture the New Being has power to transform those who are transformed by it. This implies that there is an *analogia imaginis,* namely, an analogy between the picture and the actual personal life from which it has arisen. It was this reality, when encountered by the disciples, which created the picture. And it was, and still is, this picture which mediates the transforming power of the New Being. One can compare the *analogia imaginis* suggested here with the *analogia entis*—not as a method of knowing God but as a way (actually the only way) of speaking of God. In both cases it is impossible to push behind the analogy and to state directly what can be stated only indirectly, that is, symbolically in the knowledge of God and mediated through faith in the knowledge of Jesus. But this indirect, symbolic, and mediated character of our knowledge does not diminish its truth-value. For in both cases what is given to us as material for our indirect knowledge is dependent on the object of our knowledge. The symbolic material through which we speak about God is an expression of the divine self-manifestation, and the mediated material which is given to us in the biblical picture of the Christ is the result of the reception of the New Being and its transforming power on the part of the first witnesses. The concrete biblical material is not guaranteed by faith in respect to empirical factuality; but it is guaranteed as an adequate expression of the transforming power of the New Being in Jesus as the Christ. Only in this sense does faith guarantee the biblical picture of Jesus. And it can be shown that, in all periods of the history of the church, it was this picture which created both the church and the Christian, and not a hypothetical description of what may lie behind the biblical picture. But the picture has this creative power, because the power of the New Being is expressed in and through it. This consideration leads to the distinction between an imaginary picture and a real picture. A picture imagined by the same contemporaries of Jesus would have expressed their untransformed existence and their quest for a New Being. But it would not have been the New Being itself. That is tested by its transforming power.

The word "picture" may lead to another analogy. Those who try to push behind the biblical picture to discover the "historical Jesus" with the help of the critical method try to provide a photograph (corroborated by a phonograph and, if possible, a psychograph). A good photograph is not without subjective elements, and no one would deny that every empirical description of a historical figure has such elements. The opposite attitude would be to interpret the New Testament picture as the painted projection of the experiences and ideals of the most religiously profound minds in the period of the Emperor Augustus. The idealistic style of art is analogous to this attitude. The third way is that of an "expressionist" portrait ("expressionist" used in the sense of the predominant artistic style in most periods of history—rediscovered in our period). In this approach a painter would try to enter into the deepest levels of the person with whom he deals. And he could do so only by a profound participation in the reality and the meaning of his subject matter. Only then could he paint this person in such a way that his surface traits are neither reproduced as in photography (or naturalistically imitated) nor idealized according to the painter's ideal of beauty but are used to express what the painter has experienced through his participation in the being of his subject. This third way is meant when we use the term "real picture" with reference to the Gospel records of Jesus as the Christ. With Adolf Schlatter we can say that we know nobody as well as Jesus. In contrast to all other persons, the participation in him takes place not in the realm of contingent human individuality (which can never be approached completely by any other individual) but in the realm of his own participation in God, a participation which, in spite of the mystery of every person's relation to God, has a universality in which everyone can participate. Of course, in terms of historical documentation we do know many people better than Jesus. But in terms of personal participation in his being, we do not know anyone better because his being is the New Being which is universally valid for every human being.

A very interesting argument against the position taken here must be mentioned. It is based on the common assumption that faith, by its very nature, includes an element of risk and on the question asked by this argument: Why not take the risk of historical uncertainty as well? The affirmation that Jesus is the Christ is an act of faith and consequently of daring courage. It is not an arbitrary leap into darkness but a decision in which elements of immediate participation and therefore certitude are mixed with elements of strangeness and therefore incertitude and doubt. But doubt is not the opposite of faith; it is an element of faith. Therefore, there is no faith without risk. The risk of faith is that it could affirm a wrong symbol of ultimate concern, a symbol which does not really express ultimacy (as, e.g., Dionysus or one's nation). But this risk lies in quite a different dimension from the risk of accepting uncertain historical facts. It is wrong, therefore, to consider the risk concerning uncertain historical facts as part of the risk of faith. The risk of faith is existential; it concerns the totality of our being, while the risk of historical judgments is theoretical and open to permanent scientific correction. Here are two different dimensions which should never be confused. A wrong faith can destroy the meaning of one's life; a wrong historical judgment cannot. It is misleading, therefore, to use the word "risk" for both dimensions in the same sense.

7. The Biblical Witness to Jesus as the Christ

In all respects the New Testament is the document wherein there appears the picture of Jesus as the Christ in its original and basic form. All other documents, from the Apostolic Fathers to the writings of the present-day theologians, are dependent upon this original document. In itself the New Testament is an integral part of the event which it documents. The New Testament represents the receptive side of that event and provides, as such, a witness to its factual side. If this is true, one can say that the New Testament as a whole is the basic document of the event upon which the Christian faith rests. In this respect the several parts of the New Testament agree. In other respects there is much difference. All New Testament books are united, however, in the assertion that Jesus is the Christ. It was the desire of so-called *liberal theology* to go behind the biblical records of Jesus as the Christ. In such an attempt the first three Gospels emerge as by far the most important part of the New Testament, and this is what they became in the estimation of many modern theologians. But the moment when one realizes that the Christian faith cannot be built on such a foundation, the Fourth Gospel and the Epistles become equally important with the Synoptics. One then sees that there is no conflict between them in their one decisive point of pronouncing Jesus as the Christ. The difference between the Synoptic Gospels and the other literature of the New Testament—including the Fourth Gospel—is that the former give the picture on which the assertion that Jesus is the Christ is based, while the latter give the elaboration of this assertion and its implications for Christian thought and life. This distinction is not exclusive, for it is a difference in emphasis, not in substance. Harnack was wrong, therefore, when he contrasted the message given by Jesus with the message about Jesus. There is no substantial difference between the message given by the Synoptic Jesus and the message about Jesus given in Paul's Epistles. This statement is independent of the attempts of liberal theology to deprive the first three Gospels of all Paulinian elements. Historical criticism can do that with a certain degree of probability. But the more successfully this is done, the less remains of the Synoptic picture of Jesus as the Christ. This picture and Paul's message of the Christ do not contradict each other. The New Testament witness is unanimous in its witness to Jesus as the Christ. This witness is the foundation of the Christian church.

B. THE NEW BEING IN JESUS AS THE CHRIST

1. THE NEW BEING AND THE NEW EON

According to eschatological symbolism, the Christ is the one who brings the new eon. When Peter called Jesus "the Christ," he expected the coming of a new state of things through him. This expectation is implicit in the title "Christ." But it was not fulfilled in accordance with the expectations of the disciples. The state of things, of nature as well as of history, remained unchanged, and he who was supposed to bring the new eon was destroyed by the powers of the old eon. This meant that the disciples either had to accept the breakdown of their hope or radically transform its content. They were able to choose the second way by identifying the New Being with the being of Jesus, the sacrificed. In the Synoptic records Jesus himself reconciled the messianic claim with the acceptance of a violent death. The same records show that the disciples resisted this combination. Only the experiences which are described as Easter and Pentecost created their faith in the paradoxical character of the messianic claim. It was Paul who gave the theological frame in which the paradox could be understood and justified. One approach to the solution of the problem was to state the distinction between the first and the second coming of the Christ. The new state of things will be created with the second coming, the return of the Christ in glory. In the period between the first and the second coming the New Being is present in him. He *is* the Kingdom of God. In him the eschatological expectation is fulfilled in principle. Those who participate in him participate in the New Being, though under the condition of man's existential predicament and, therefore, only fragmentarily and by anticipation.

New Being is essential being under the conditions of existence, conquering the gap between essence and existence. For the same idea Paul uses the term "new creature," calling those who are "in" Christ "new creatures." "In" is the preposition of participation; he who participates in the newness of being which is in Christ has become a new creature. It is a creative act by which this happens. Inasmuch as Jesus as the Christ is a creation of the divine Spirit, according to Synoptic theology, so is he who participates in the Christ made into a new creature by the Spirit. The estrangement of his existential from his essential being is conquered in principle, i.e., in power and as a beginning. The term "New Being," as used here, points directly to the cleavage between essential and existential being—and is the restorative principle of the whole of this theological system. The New Being is new in so far as it is the undistorted manifestation of essential being within and under the conditions of existence. It is new in two respects: it is new in contrast to the merely potential character of essential being; and it is new over against the estranged character of existential being. It is actual, conquering the estrangement of actual existence.

There are other ways of expressing the same idea. The New Being is new in so far as it is the conquest of the situation under the law—which is the old situation. The law is man's essential being standing against his existence, commanding and judging it. In so far as his essential being is taken into his existence and actualized in it, the law has ceased to be law for him. Where there is New Being, there is no commandment and no judgment. If, therefore, we call Jesus as the Christ the New Being, we say with Paul that the Christ is the end of the law.

In terms of the eschatological symbolism it can also be said that Christ is the end of existence. He is the end of existence lived in estrangement, conflicts, and self-destruction. The biblical idea that the hope of mankind for a new reality is fulfilled in Jesus as the Christ is an immediate consequence of the assertion that in him the New Being is present. His appearance is "realized eschatology" (Dodd). Of course, it is fulfilment "in principle," it is the manifestation of the power and the beginning of fulfilment. But it is realized eschatology in so far as no other principle of fulfilment can be expected. In him has appeared what fulfilment qualitatively means.

With the same qualification, one can say that in him history has come to an end, namely, that its preparatory period has reached its aim. Nothing qualitatively new in the dimension of the ultimate can be produced by history which is not implicitly present in the New Being in Jesus as the Christ. The assertion that the Christ is the "end" of history seems to be absurd in the light of the history of the last two thousand years. But it is not absurd if one understands the double sense of "end," namely, "finish" and "aim." In the sense of "finish," history has not yet come to an end. It goes on and shows all the characteristics of existential estrangement. It is the place in which finite freedom is at work, producing existential distortion and the great ambiguities of life. In the sense of "aim," history has come to an intrinsic end qualitatively, namely, in the appearance of the New Being as a historical reality. But, quantitatively considered, the actualization of the New Being within history is drawn into the distortions and ambiguities of man's historical predicament. This oscillation between "already" and "not yet" is the experience which is symbolized in the tension between the first and second comings of the Christ; it belongs inseparably to the Christian existence.

2. The New Being Appearing in a Personal Life

The New Being has appeared in a personal life, and for humanity it could not have appeared in any other way; for the potentialities of being are completely actual in personal life alone. Only a person, within our experience, is a fully developed self, confronting a world to which it belongs at the same time. Only in a person are the polarities of being complete. Only a person is completely individualized, and for just this reason he is able to participate without limits in his world. Only a person has an unlimited power of self-transcendence, and for just this reason he has the complete structure, the structure of rationality. Only a person has freedom, including all its characteristics, and for just this reason he alone has destiny. Only the person is finite freedom, which gives him the power of contradicting himself and returning to himself. Of no other being can all this be said. And only in such a being can the New Being appear. Only where existence is most radically existence—in him who is finite freedom—can existence be conquered.

But what happens to man happens implicitly to all realms of life, for in man all levels of being are present. He belongs to physical, biological, and psychological realms and is subject to their manifold degrees and the various relations between them. For this reason the philosophers of the Renaissance called man the "microcosmos." He is a universe in himself. What happens in him happens, therefore, by mutual universal participation. This, of course, is said in qualitative, not quantitative terms. Quantitatively speaking, the universe is largely indifferent to what happens in man. Qualitatively speaking, nothing happens in man that does not have a bearing on the elements which constitute the universe. This gives cosmic significance to the person and confirms the insight that only in a personal life can the New Being manifest itself.

3. The Expressions of the New Being in Jesus as the Christ

Jesus as the Christ is the bearer of the New Being in the totality of his being, not in any special expressions of it. It is his being that makes him the Christ because his being has the quality of the New Being beyond the split of essential and existential being. From this it follows that neither his words, deeds, or sufferings nor what is called his "inner life" make him the Christ. They are all expressions of the New Being, which is the quality of his being, and this, his being, precedes and transcends all its expressions. This assertion can serve as a critical tool against several inadequate ways of describing his character as the Christ.

The first expression of the being of Jesus as the Christ is his words. The word is the bearer of spiritual life. The importance of the spoken word for the religion of the New Testament cannot be overestimated. The words of Jesus, to cite but two examples of many, are called "words of eternal life," and discipleship is made dependent upon "holding to his words." And he himself is called "the Word." It is just this last instance that shows it is not his words which make him the Christ but his being. This is metaphorically called "the Word" because it is the final self-manifestation of God to humanity. His being, which is called "the Word," expresses itself *also* in his words. But, as the Word, he is more than all the words he has spoken. This assertion is the basic criticism of a theology which separates the words of Jesus from his being and makes him into a teacher, preacher, or prophet. This theological tendency, as old as the church, is represented by ancient and modern rationalism. It came to the foreground in the so-called "liberal theology" of the nineteenth century. But its theological significance is surpassed by its influence on the popular mind. It plays a tremendous role in the piety of daily life, particularly in those groups for whom Christianity has become a system of conventional rules commanded by a divine teacher. In educational contexts particularly, one speaks of "the teachings of Jesus" and makes them the basis for religious instruction. This is not necessarily wrong, because the term "teaching of Jesus"—better used in the singular—can cover his prophetic message of the presence of the Kingdom of God within himself. Ordinarily, the term is used (mostly in the plural) for doctrinal statements of Jesus about God, man, and, above all, what is demanded of man. If used in this sense, the term "the teachings of Jesus," makes him into another person, who gives doctrinal and ethical laws. This view is obviously a relapse to the legalistic type of self-salvation, the appearance of the New Being in the Christ. It is the replacement of Jesus as the Christ by the religious and moral teacher called Jesus of Nazareth. Against such theology and its popularized application, one must hold to the principle that "being precedes speaking." The words of Jesus have the power to create the New Being only because Jesus as the Christ *is* the Word, and only in the power of the New Being can his words be transformed into reality.

The second expression of the New Being in Jesus as the Christ is his deeds. They also have been separated from his being and made into examples to be imitated. He is not considered to be a lawgiver but as himself being the new law. There is much justification for this idea. If Jesus as the Christ represents the essential unity between God and man appearing under the conditions of existential estrangement, every human being is, by this very fact, asked to take on the "form of the Christ." Being Christlike means participating fully in the New Being present in him. In this sense the Christ *is* the new law, and equality with him is implictly demanded. But if this is interpreted as the command to imitate the Christ, wrong consequences are inescapable. *Imitatio Christi* is often understood as the attempt to transform one's life into a copy of the life of Jesus, including the concrete traits of the biblical picture. But this contradicts the meaning of these traits as parts of his being within the picture of Jesus the Christ. These traits are supposed to make translucent the New Being, which is his being. As such, they point beyond their contingent character and are not instances to imitate. If they are used in this way, they lose their transparency and become ritualistic or ascetic prescriptions. If the word "imitation" is used at all in this context, it should indicate that we, *in* our concreteness, are asked to participate in the New Being and to be transformed by it, not beyond, but within, the contingencies of our life. Not his actions but the being out of which his actions come makes him the Christ. If he is understood as the new law and the object of imitation, it is almost unavoidable that the new law will take on the character of copying or of imitation. Protestantism, therefore, rightly hesitated to use these terms after their patent abuse in Roman Catholicism. And Protestantism should resist pietistic and revivalist attempts to reintroduce those elements which separate the actions of the Christ from his being.

The third expression of the New Being in Jesus as the Christ is his suffering. It includes his violent death and is a consequence of the inescapable conflict between the forces of existential estrangement and the bearer of that by which existence is conquered. Only by taking suffering and death upon himself could Jesus be the Christ, because only in this way could he participate completely in existence and conquer every force of estrangement which tried to dissolve his unity with God. The significance of the Cross in the New Testament picture of Jesus as the Christ induced orthodox theologians to separate both suffering and death from his being and to make these his decisive function as the Christ within the frame of a sacrificial theory. This is partially justifiable; for, without the continuous sacrifice of himself as a particular individual under the conditions of existence to himself as the bearer of the New Being, he could not have been the Christ. He proves and confirms his character as the Christ in the sacrifice of himself as Jesus to himself as the Christ. But it is not justifiable to separate this sacrificial function from his being, of which it is actually an expression. It has, however, been done in theories of atonement, such as that of Anselm of Canterbury. The sacrificial death of the Christ is, for him, the *opus supererogatorium* which makes it possible for God to overcome the conflict between his love and his wrath. This is not the place to deal with the Anselmian theory of atonement as such; but we must deal with the consequences which that theory has for the interpretation of Christ. His "divine nature" is always presupposed, and in this sense his character as the bearer of the New Being is affirmed (in terms of the christological dogma). But his being is treated only as a presupposition of his death and of its effect on God and man. It is not treated as *the* significant factor, as that which makes him the Christ and as that of which the necessary consequences are suffering and death. The suffering on the Cross is not something additional which can be separated from the appearance of the eternal God-Manhood under the conditions of existence; it is an inescapable implication of this appearance. Like his words and his deeds, the suffering of Jesus as the Christ is an expression of the New Being in him. It is an astonishing abstraction when Anselm states that Jesus owed God active obedience but not suffering and death—as if the unity between God and the Christ could have been maintained under the conditions of existential estrangement without the continuous acceptance of his suffering and having to die.

With these considerations in mind, we must evaluate the rationalistic separation of the *words* of Jesus from his being, the pietistic separation of his *deeds* from his being, and the orthodox separation of the *suffering* of Jesus from his being. We must understand his being as the New Being and its expressions as manifestations of him as the Christ.

An attempt to think along this line was made by theologians such as W. Herrmann, who tried to penetrate into the inner life of Jesus, into his relation to God, men, and himself. It has been done in connection with the search for the "historical Jesus." It is certainly justifiable to say that if the New Being is actualized in a personal life, it is actual in those movements which cannot be externalized, even though they influence all expressions of the person. The only way of approaching the inner life of a person is through conclusions drawn from these expressions. Such conclusions are always questionable and especially so in the case of Jesus. This is so not only because of the character of our records but also because the uniqueness of his being makes conclusions from analogy extremely doubtful. Significantly, the biblical reports about Jesus do not psychologize. More correctly, one could say that they ontologize. They speak about the divine Spirit in him or about his unity with the Father. They speak about his resistance to demonic temptations, about his patient, yet critical, love toward disciples and sinners. They speak of his experience of loneliness and of meaninglessness and of his anxiety about the violent death which threatened him. But all this is neither psychology nor the description of a character structure. Nor is it an attempt to penetrate into the inner life of Jesus. Our records do not give a psychological description of his development, piety, or inner conflicts. They show only the presence of the New Being in him under the conditions of existence. Of course, everything that happens in a person happens in and through his psychological structure. But, by recording his anxiety about having to die, the New Testament writers show his total participation in human finitude. Not only do they show the expression of a special form of anxiety, but they also show his conquest of anxiety. And, without that conquest, he could not have been the Messiah. In all cases it is an occasion of the encounter of the New Being with the forces of estrangement, not some specific psychological behavior which is involved. The attempt, then, to penetrate into the inner life of Jesus in order to describe his messianic qualities must be considered a failure, although it is an attempt to deal directly with the New Being in Jesus as the Christ.

At this point it may be recalled that the term "being," when applied to God as an initial statement about him, was interpreted as the "power of being" or, negatively expressed, as the power to resist non-being. In an analogous way the term "New Being," when applied to Jesus as the Christ, points to the power in him which conquers existential estrangement or, negatively expressed, to the power of resisting the forces of estrangement. To experience the New Being in Jesus as the Christ means to experience the power in him which has conquered existential estrangement in himself and in everyone who participates in him. "Being," if used for God or divine manifestations, is the power of being or, negatively expressed, the power of conquering non-being. The word "being" points to the fact that this power is not a matter of someone's good will but that it is a gift which precedes or determines the character of every act of the will. In this sense, one can say that the concept of the New Being re-establishes the meaning of grace. While "realism" was in danger of misinterpreting grace in a magical form, "nominalism" was in danger of completely losing the concept of grace. Without an understanding of "being" and "the power of being," it is impossible to speak meaningfully of grace.

4. THE NEW BEING IN JESUS AS THE CHRIST AS THE CONQUEST
   OF ESTRANGEMENT

   a) The New Being in the Christ and the marks of estrangement.—
In all its concrete details the biblical picture of Jesus as the Christ confirms his character as the bearer of the New Being or as the one in whom the conflict between the essential unity of God and man and man's existential estrangement is overcome. Point by point, not only in the Gospel records but also in the Epistles, this picture of Jesus as the

Christ contradicts the marks of estrangement which we have elaborated in the analysis of man's existential predicament. This is not surprising, since the analysis was partly dependent on the confrontation of man's existential predicament with the image of the New Being in the Christ. According to the biblical picture of Jesus as the Christ, there are, in spite of all tensions, no traces of estrangement between him and God and consequently between him and himself and between him and his world (in its essential nature). The paradoxical character of his being consists in the fact that, although he has only finite freedom under the conditions of time and space, he is not estranged from the ground of his being. There are no traces of unbelief, namely, the removal of his personal center from the divine center which is the subject of his infinite concern. Even in the extreme situation of despair about his messianic work, he cries to his God who has forsaken him. In the same way the biblical picture shows no trace of *hubris* or self-elevation in spite of his awareness of his messianic vocation. In the critical moment in which Peter first calls him the Christ, he combines the acceptance of this title with the acceptance of his violent death, including the warning to his disciples not to make his messianic function public. This is equally emphasized in Paul's christological hymn, Philippians, chapter 2, where he combines the divine form of the transcendent Christ with the acceptance of the form of a servant. The Fourth Gospel provides the theological foundation for this in the passage ascribed to Jesus: "He who believes in me does not believe in me, but in Him who has sent me." Nor is there any trace of concupiscence in the picture. This point is stressed in the story of the temptation in the desert. Here the desires for food, acknowledgment, and unlimited power are used by Satan as the possible weak spots in the Christ. As the Messiah, he could fulfil these desires. But then he would have been demonic and would have ceased to be the Christ.

The conquest of estrangement by the New Being in Jesus as the Christ should not be described in the term "the sinlessness of Jesus." This is a negative term and is used in the New Testament merely to show his victory over the messianic temptation (Letter to the Hebrews) to set forth the dignity of him who is the Christ in refusing to sacrifice himself by subjection to the destructive consequences of estrangement. There is, in fact, no enumeration of special sins which he did not commit, nor is there a day-by-day description of the ambiguities of life in which he proved to be unambiguously good. He rejects the term "good" as applicable to himself in isolation from God and puts the problem in the right place, namely, the uniqueness of his relation to God. His goodness is goodness only in so far as he participates in the goodness of God. Jesus, like every man, is finite freedom. Without that, he would not be equal with mankind and could not be the Christ. God alone is above freedom and destiny. In him alone the tensions of this and all other polarities are eternally conquered; in Jesus they are actual. The term "sinlessness" is a rationalization of the biblical picture of him who has conquered the forces of existential estrangement within existence. As early as in the New Testament, such rationalizations appear in several places, as, for example, in some miracle stories—the story of the empty tomb, the virgin birth, the bodily ascendance, etc. Whether it appears in stories or concepts, their character is always the same. Something positive is affirmed concerning the Christ (and, later on, of other biblical figures) and is interpreted in terms of negations which, in principle, are open to empirical verification. In this way a religious statement of existential-symbolic character is transformed into a theoretical statement of rational-objectifying character.

The biblical picture is thoroughly positive in showing a threefold emphasis: first, the complete finitude of the Christ; second, the reality of the temptations growing out of it; third, the victory over these temptations in so far as the defeat in them would have disrupted his relation to God and ruined his messianic vocation. Beyond these three points, which are based on the actual experience of the disciples, no inquiry is possible and meaningful, and especially not if sin is used in the singular, as it should be.

b) *The reality of the temptations of Christ.*—Since Jesus as the Christ is finite freedom, he also confronts real temptation. Possibility is itself temptation. And Jesus would not represent the essential unity between God and man (Eternal God-Manhood) without the possibility of real temptation. A monophysitic tendency, which runs through all church history, including theologians and popular Christianity, has tacitly led many to deny that the temptations of the Christ were serious. They could not tolerate the full humanity of Jesus as the Christ, his finite freedom, and, with it, the possibility of defeat in temptation. Unintentionally, they deprived Jesus of his real finitude and attributed a divine transcendence to him above freedom and destiny. The church was right, though never fully successful, in resisting the monophysitic distortion of the picture of Jesus as the Christ.

However, if one accepts the affirmation that the biblical story points to serious temptations, one must face a problem which is important for the doctrine of man generally, including the doctrine of the transition from essence to existence. Man's fall from dreaming innocence to self-actualization and estrangement poses the same anthropological problem as the victory of Christ over existential estrangement. One must ask: Under what conditions is a temptation serious? Is not one of the conditions an actual desire toward that which has the power to tempt? But if there is such a desire, is there not estrangement prior to a decision to succumb or not to succumb to the temptation? There is no doubt that under the conditions of existence this is the human situation. From the very beginning of life our desire pushes ahead, and possibilities appear. These possibilities become temptation if a prohibition (as in the paradise story) forces one into deliberation and decision. The question, then, is how to evaluate the desire, be it that of Adam with respect to knowledge and power, as in the paradise story, or be it that of Jesus with respect to glory and power in the temptation story. The answer can be given in terms of our analysis of concupiscence. The difference between the natural self-transcendence, which includes the desire for reunion with everything, and the distorted concupiscence, which does not want reunion with anything but the exploitation of everything through power and pleasure, is one which is decisive for the evaluation of desire in the state of temptation. Without desire, there is no temptation, but the temptation is that desire will become changed into concupiscence. The prohibition lays down the conditions which would prevent the transition from desire to concupiscence. In the paradise story these conditions are not given. It is not indicated that the desire for knowledge and power is justified if it does not become concupiscence. One can only derive an indication from his relation to the fruits of life to which Adam first is admitted and then excluded: he shall not have eternity without God. In the same way, one may draw the analogy that he shall not have knowledge without God. The desire in itself is not bad (the fruit is good to eat); but the conditions of its lawful fulfilment are not kept, and so the act of eating becomes an act of concupiscence. In the story of Jesus' temptations, the conditions of a lawful fulfilment of his desires are at least indicated. They are given in the Old Testament quotations with which Jesus rejects Satan. And we find exactly the condition which appears in the paradise story: it is wrong to have the objects of justified desires without God. Jesus could have had them, but it would have meant surrendering his messianic quality.

The distinction between desire and concupiscence is the first step toward the solution of the problem raised by the seriousness of the temptations of Christ.

The second step must deal with the question of how desire is possible at all in the state of an unbroken unity with God. The word "desire" is the expression of unfulfilment. But religious literature is replete with descriptions of persons who are in unity with God and find complete fulfilment. If, however, man in essential unity with God (Adam) and man in actual unity with God under the conditions of existence (the Christ) are tempted on the basis of their desire for finite fulfilment, then desire and unity with God cannot contradict each other (this would include the statement that *eros* and *agape* cannot contradict each other). Positively expressed, this means that life in unity with God, like all life, is determined by the polarity of dynamics and form and, as such, is never without the risk implied in the tensions between dynamics and form. The unity with God is not the negation of the desire for reunion of the finite with the finite. But where there is unity with God, there the finite is not desired alongside this unity but within it. The temptation which is rooted in desire is that the finite is desired alongside God or that desire becomes concupiscence. This is the rationale which makes the object of desire a serious temptation even in Christ.

Yet we must take a third step in order to answer the questions arising from the reality of the temptations of Jesus. The suspicion of considerations like the preceding stem from the fear that they make the rejection of the temptations of Jesus a matter of contingency. If this were the case, the salvation of mankind would be dependent on the contingent decision of an individual man. But such an argument does not take into consideration the polar unity of freedom and destiny. The universality of existential estrangement and the uniqueness of the victory over estrangement are both matters of freedom as well as of destiny. The decision of the Christ against succumbing to the temptations is an act of his finite freedom and, as such, analogous to a decision by anyone who is finite freedom, i.e., by any man. As a free decision, it is an act of his total personality and of the center of his own self. At the same time it is, as in anyone who is finite freedom, a consequence of his destiny. His freedom was imbedded in his destiny. Freedom without destiny is mere contingency, and destiny without freedom is mere necessity. But human freedom and, consequently, the freedom of Jesus as the Christ are united with destiny and therefore are neither contingency nor necessity.

The element of destiny in the picture of the Christ is taken very seriously in the New Testament. His heredity and bodily existence are matters of speculation and research into the Synoptic Gospels. He is not isolated; he is the central link in the chain of divine revelations. The importance of his mother is not diminished by the fact that she does not understand him. Many factors which help determine the destiny of a man are mentioned in the biblical records. What happens to him is always a consequence of his destiny as well as an act of his freedom. In the many references of the New Testament to the prophecies of the Old Testament, the element of destiny is clearly expressed. The appearance of Jesus as the Christ and his resistance to the attempts to deprive him of his Christ-character are both acts of decision by himself and results of a divine destiny. Beyond this unity we cannot go, either in the case of Jesus or in the case of man universally.

This insight answers the anxious question of whether the salvation of mankind is due to the contingent decision of an individual man (freedom in the sense of indeterminism) in the negative. The decisions of Jesus in which he resisted real temptation, like every human decision, stand under the directing creativity of God (providence). And God's directing creativity in the case of man works through his freedom. Man's destiny is determined *by* the divine creativity, but *through* man's self-determination, that is, through his finite freedom. In this respect the "history of salvation" and the "history of the Savior" are ultimately determined in the same way as history is generally and as the history of every individual man. This refers also to the state of estrangement in which mankind finds itself. Nobody can seriously defend the absurd idea that the universal cause of the human predicament was contingent upon the wrong decision of an individual man. In the same way the appearance of the Christ is at the same time freedom and destiny and is determined by God's directing creativity. There is no undetermined contingency in the negative and the positive situation of mankind, but there is the unity of freedom and destiny under God's directing creativity.

c) *The marks of his finitude.*—The seriousness of the temptation of the Christ is based on the fact that he is finite freedom. The degree to which the biblical picture of Jesus as the Christ stresses his finitude is remarkable. As a finite being, he is subject to the contingency of everything that is not by itself but is "thrown" into existence. He has to die, and he experiences the anxiety of having to die. This anxiety is described by the evangelists in the most vivid way. It is not relieved by the expectation of resurrection "after three days," or by the ecstasy of a substitutional self-sacrifice, or even by the ideal of the heroism of wise men such as Socrates. Like every man, he experiences the threat of the victory of non-being over being, as, for instance, in the limits of the span of life given to him. As in the case of all finite beings, he experiences the lack of a definite place. From his birth on, he appears strange and homeless in his world. He has bodily, social, and mental insecurity, is subject to want, and is expelled by his nation. In relation to other persons, his finitude is manifest in his loneliness, both in respect to the masses and in respect to his relatives and disciples. He struggles to make them understand, but during his life he never succeeds. His frequent desire for solitude shows that many hours of his daily life were filled with various finite concerns produced by his encounter with the world. At the same time, he is deeply affected by the misery of the masses and of everyone who turns to him. He accepts them, even though he will be rejected by them. He experiences all the tensions which follow from the self-relatedness of every finite person and proves the impossibility of penetrating into the center of anyone else.

In relation to reality as such, including things and persons, he is subject to uncertainty in judgment, risks of error, the limits of power, and the vicissitudes of life. The Fourth Gospel says of him that he *is* truth, but this does not mean that he *has* omniscience or absolute certainty. He *is* the truth in so far as his being—the New Being in him—conquers the untruth of existential estrangement. But being the truth is not the same as knowing the truth about all finite objects and situations. Finitude implies openness to error, and error belongs to the participation of the Christ in man's existential predicament. Error is evident in his ancient conception of the universe, his judgments about men, his interpretation of the historical moment, his eschatological imagination.

If we finally look at his relation to himself, we can refer again to what was said about the seriousness of his temptations. They presuppose want and desire. We can also refer to his doubt about his own work, as in his hesitation to accept the messianic title, and, above all, his feeling of having been left alone by God without God's expected interference on the Cross.

All this belongs to the description of the finitude of Jesus as the Christ and has its place within the totality of his picture. It is *one* element along with others; but it must be emphasized against those who attribute to him a hidden omnipotence, omniscience, omnipresence, and eternity. The latter take away the seriousness of his finitude and with it the reality of his participation in existence.

d) His participation in the tragic element of existence.—Every encounter with reality, whether with situations, groups, or individuals, is burdened with practical and theoretical uncertainty. This uncertainty is caused not only by the finitude of the individual but also by the ambiguity of that which a person encounters. Life is marked by ambiguity, and one of the ambiguities is that of greatness and tragedy (which I shall deal with in Vol. III). This raises the question of how the bearer of the New Being is involved in the tragic element of life. What is his relation to the ambiguity of tragic guilt? What is his relation to the tragic consequences of his being, including his actions and decisions, for those who are with him or who are against him and for those who are neither one nor the other?

The first and historically most important example in this area is the conflict of Jesus with the leaders of his nation. The ordinary Christian view is that their hostility toward him is unambiguously their religious and moral guilt. They decided against him, although they could have decided for him. But this "could" is just the problem. It removes the tragic element which universally belongs to existence. It places the leaders out of the context of humanity and makes them into representatives of unambiguous evil. But there is no unambiguous evil. This is acknowledged by Jesus when he refers to the traditions and when he expresses that he belongs to the "house of Israel." Although continuously persecuted by the Jews, Paul witnesses to their zeal to fulfil the law of God. The Pharisees were the pious ones of their time, and they represented the law of God, the preparatory revelation, without which the final revelation could not have happened. If Christians deny the tragic element in the encounter between Jesus and the Jews (and analogously between Paul and the Jews), they are guilty of a profound injustice. And this injustice early produced a Christian anti-Judaism which is one of the permanent sources of modern anti-Semitism. It is regrettable that even today much Christian instruction is consciously or unconsciously responsible for this kind of anti-Jewish feeling. This can be changed only if we frankly admit that the conflict between Jesus and his enemies was a tragic one. This means that Jesus was involved in the tragic element of guilt, in so far as he made his enemies inescapably guilty. This element of guilt did not touch his personal relation to God. It did not produce estrangement. It did not split his personal center. But it is an expression of his participation in existential estrangement, and its implication, namely, the ambiguity of creation and destruction. It was a profound insight into the tragic element of guilt when Kierkegaard questioned the right of anyone to let himself be killed for the truth. He who does so must know that he becomes tragically responsible for the guilt of those who kill him.

Many embarrassing questions have been asked about the relation of Jesus and Judas—from the New Testament period on. One of the problems in the stories of the betrayal of Judas is indicated by Jesus himself. On the one hand, he asserts the providential necessity—the fulfilment of the prophecies—of the deed of Judas, and, on the other hand, he emphasizes the immensity of the personal guilt of Judas. The tragic and the moral elements in the guilt of Judas are equally stated. But, besides this more universal element of tragedy in the guilt of Judas, there is a special one. The betrayal presupposes that Judas belonged to the intimate group of disciples. And this could not have been the case without the will of Jesus. Implicitly, we have already referred to this point when we spoke of the errors in judgment which cannot be separated from finite existence. Explicitly, we must say that, as the story stands in the records (and this is the only question we are dealing with here), the innocent one becomes tragically guilty in respect to the very one who contributes to his own death. One should not try to escape these consequences, if one takes seriously the participation in the ambiguities of life, on the part of him who is the bearer of the New Being. If Jesus as the Christ were seen as a God walking on earth, he would be neither finite nor involved in tragedy. His judgment would be ultimate, and that means an unambiguous judgment. But, according to biblical symbolism, this is a matter of his "second coming" and is therefore connected with the transformation of reality as a whole. The Christ of the biblical picture takes upon himself the consequences of his tragic involvement in existence. The New Being in him has eternal significance also for those who caused his death, including Judas.

e) His permanent unity with God.—The conquest of existential estrangement in the New Being, which is the being of the Christ, does not remove finitude and anxiety, ambiguity and tragedy; but it does have the character of taking the negativities of existence into unbroken unity with God. The anxiety about having to die is not removed; it is taken into participation in the "will of God," i.e., in his directing creativity. His homelessness and insecurity with respect to a physical, social, and mental place are not diminished but rather increased to the last moment. Yet they are accepted in the power of a participation in a "transcendent place," which in actuality is no place but the eternal ground of every place and of every moment of time. His loneliness and his frustrated attempts in trying to be received by those to whom he came do not suddenly end in a final success; they are taken into the divine acceptance of that which rejects God, into the vertical line of the uniting love which is effective where the horizontal line from being to being is barred. Out of his unity with God he has unity with those who are separated from him and from one another by finite self-relatedness and existential self-seclusion. Both error and doubt equally are not removed but are taken into the participation in the divine life and thus indirectly into the divine omniscience. Both error and truth are taken into the transcendent truth. Therefore, we do not find symptoms of repression of doubt in the picture of Jesus as the Christ. Those who are not able to elevate their doubts into the truth which transcends every finite truth must repress them. They perforce become fanatical. Yet no traces of fanaticism are present in the biblical picture. Jesus does not claim absolute certitude for a finite conviction. He rejects the fanatical attitude of the disciples toward those who do not follow him. In the power of a certitude which transcends certitude and incertitude in matters of religion as well as secular life, he accepts incertitude as an element of finiteness. This also refers to the doubt about his own work —a doubt which breaks through most intensively on the Cross but still does not destroy his unity with God.

This is the picture of the New Being in Jesus as the Christ. It is not the picture of a divine-human automaton without serious temptation, real struggle, or tragic involvement in the ambiguities of life. Instead of that, it is the picture of a personal life which is subjected to all the consequences of existential estrangement but wherein estrangement is conquered in himself and a permanent unity is kept with God. Into this unity he accepts the negativities of existence without removing them. This is done by transcending them in the power of this unity. This is the New Being as it appears in the biblical picture of Jesus as the Christ.

5. The Historical Dimension of the New Being

There is no personal life without the encounter with other persons within a community, and there is no community without the historical dimension of past and future. This is clearly indicated in the biblical picture of Jesus as the Christ. Although his personal life is considered as the criterion by which past and future are judged, it is not an isolated life, and the New Being, which is the quality of his own being, is not restricted to his being. This refers to the community out of which he comes and to the preparatory manifestations of the New Being within it; it refers to the community which he creates and to the received manifestations of the New Being in it. The New Testament records take very seriously the descent of Jesus from the life of bearers of the preparatory revelation. The otherwise questionable and contradictory lists of the ancestors of Jesus have this symbolic value, as do the symbol "Son of David" (see above) and the interest in the figure of his mother. These are all symbols of the historical dimension of the past. In the selection of the Twelve Apostles, the past of the twelve tribes of Israel is symbolically connected with the future of the church. And, without the reception of Jesus as the Christ by the church, he could not have become the Christ, because he would not have brought the New Being to anyone. While the Synoptic picture is especially interested in the direction of the past, the Fourth Gospel is predominantly interested in the direction toward the future. Clearly, however, the biblical picture is not responsible for a theology which, in the name of the "uniqueness" of Jesus as the Christ, cuts him off from everything before the year 1 and after the year 30. In this way the continuity of the divine self-manifestation through history is denied not only for the pre-Christian past but also for the Christian present and future. This tends to cut off the contemporary Christian of today from direct connection with the New Being in Christ. He is asked to jump over the millennia to the years "1 through 30" and to subject himself to the event upon which Christianity is based. But this jump is an illusion because the very fact that he is a Christian and that he calls Jesus the Christ is based on the continuity through history of the power of the New Being. No anti-Catholic bias should prevent Protestant theologians from acknowledging this fact.

Although appearing in a personal life, the New Being has a spatial breadth in the community of the New Being and a temporal dimension in the history of the New Being. The appearance of the Christ in an individual person presupposes the community out of which he came and the community which he creates. Of course, the criterion of both is the picture of Jesus as the Christ; but, without them, this criterion never could have appeared.

6. Conflicting Elements in the Picture of Jesus as the Christ

In the preceding sections we spoke of *the* picture of Jesus as the Christ and neglected the differences and contrasts in the biblical picture. The question now must be asked whether, in fact, there is such a unified picture in the New Testament or whether the conflicting views of the different writers of the New Testament make the painting of such a picture impossible. The question first demands a historical, then a systematic, answer. The historical answer has been partly given by the earlier statement that all parts of the New Testament agree in their assertion that Jesus is the Christ. This is necessarily so because the New Testament is the book of the community whose foundation is the acceptance of Jesus as the Christ. But the question is not fully answered by this statement; for there are different, and somehow contrasting, ways of interpreting the assertion that Jesus is the Christ. One can emphasize the participation of the New Being in the conditions of existence or the victory of the New Being over the conditions of existence. Obviously, the first is the Synoptic, the second the Johannine, emphasis. The question here is not whether one can produce a harmonious historical picture by a combination of both pictures. Historical research has answered this question almost unanimously in the negative. But the question is whether such contrasts, after they have become conscious to the mind of the faithful, can obstruct the impact of the biblical picture of Jesus as the bearer of the New Being. In the case of the contrast between the Synoptic emphasis on the participation of Jesus in the negativities of existence and the Johannine emphasis on the victory of the Christ over these negativities, one can, still in descriptive terms, say that the difference does not lead to an exclusion of the contrasting element. There are stories and symbols of the glory of Jesus as the Christ in the Synoptics, and stories and symbols of the suffering of Jesus as the Christ in John. Nevertheless, the systematic question is unavoidable.

The same is true of a contrast which largely overlaps that between the general mood of the Synoptics and John, namely, that between the kingdom-centered sayings of Jesus in the Synoptics and the Christ-centered nature of his sayings in John. The self-consciousness expressed in the two kinds of records seems absolutely contradictory. Here also a preliminary descriptive answer can be given. The Synoptics are not without expressions of the messianic self-consciousness of Jesus. Above all, they have no word in which Jesus identifies himself with the estrangement of humanity. He enters it and takes the tragic and self-destructive consequences upon himself, but he does not identify himself with it. Of course, the Synoptic Jesus could not speak about himself in the direct and open way in which the Johannine Christ does. But it belongs to the character of the one whose communion with God is unbroken that he feel the distance between himself and the others in whom this is not the case. Nevertheless, the contrast between the two kinds of speaking is so great that it creates a systematic problem.

A third problem appears in both the Synoptics and John. It is the way in which Jesus places himself in the eschatological framework. There are differences on this point in the consecutive levels of the Synoptic tradition as well as in the Fourth Gospel. In the Synoptics, Jesus sometimes appears merely as the prophetic announcer of the kingdom to come and sometimes as the central figure within the eschatological drama. He has to die and be resurrected for the sins of the people; he fulfils the eschatological prophecies of the Old Testament; he will return on the clouds of the sky and judge the world; he will eat the eschatological meal with his disciples. In John he sometimes repeats these eschatological statements; sometimes he transforms them into statements about eschatological processes which happen in his presence in judgment and salvation. Again one must say that neither in John nor in the Synoptics are the contrasts exclusive; but they are strong enough to demand systematic consideration.

The astonishing fact that these contrasts have not been felt over hundreds of years is due largely to the predominant influence of the Christ-picture of the Fourth Gospel in association with the cryptomonophysitic trend of the church. For Luther it is still the "main gospel," in spite of his emphasis on the lowliness of the Christ. Like most other Christians, he read the words of the Synoptic Jesus Christ as if they were the words of the Johannine Christ Jesus, in spite of the literal incompatibility. This situation no longer exists; the contrasts are seen by many Christians, and they cannot be asked to close their eyes.

The answer is that one must distinguish between the symbolic frame in which the picture of Jesus as the Christ appears and the substance in which the power of the New Being is present. We have enumerated and discussed the different symbols in which the fact "Jesus" was interpreted (of which "the Christ" is one). These interpretations are not additions to what otherwise is a finished presentation of the picture; they are the all-decisive frame within which the presentation is given. The symbol "Son of Man," for example, agrees with the eschatological frame; the symbol of the "Messiah" agrees with the passages in which the healing and preaching activity of Jesus are reported; the symbol "Son of God" and the conceptual symbol "Logos" agree with the Johannine style of speech and action. But in all cases the substance is untouched. It shines through as the power of the New Being in a threefold color: first and decisively, as the undisrupted unity of the center of his being with God; second, as the serenity and majesty of him who preserves this unity against all the attacks coming from estranged existence; and, third, as the self-surrendering love which represents and actualizes the divine love in taking the existential self-destruction upon himself. There is no passage in the Gospels—or, for that matter, in the Epistles—which takes away the power of this threefold manifestation of the New Being in the biblical picture of Jesus as the Christ.

C. VALUATION OF THE CHRISTOLOGICAL DOGMA

1. The Nature and Function of the Christological Dogma

The christological problem started with the quest for the New Being, i.e., when men became aware of their existential predicament and asked whether their predicament could be overcome through a new state of reality. In an anticipatory way the christological problem appeared in the prophetic and apocalyptic expectations associated with the Messiah or the Son of Man. The foundations for a formulated Christology were provided by the way the writers of the New Testament applied symbols to Jesus, whom they called "the Christ." Such symbols have been enumerated in our discussion of historical research into biblical literature. We have discussed the symbols—Son of Man, Son of God, the Christ. the Logos—in four steps, of which the last was the literalistic distortion of these symbols. This danger—which is always present in Christianity —was one of the reasons why the early church began to interpret the christological symbols in conceptual terms available through the work of Greek philosophy. Better for this purpose than any of the others was the symbol of the Logos, which, by its very nature, is a conceptual symbol having both religious and philosophical roots. Consequently, the Christology of the early church became Logos-Christology. It is unfair to criticize the Church Fathers for their use of Greek concepts. There were no other available conceptual expressions of man's cognitive encounter with his world. Whether or not these concepts were adequate to the interpretation of the Christian message remains a permanent question of theology. But it is wrong to reject a priori the use of Greek concepts by the early church. There was no alternative.

The dogmatic work of the early church centers in the creation of the christological dogma. All other doctrinal statements—above all, those concerning God and man, the Spirit, and the Trinity—provide the presuppositions, or are the consequences, of the christological dogma. The baptismal confession that Jesus is the Christ is the text of which the christological dogma is the commentary. The basic attacks on the Christian dogma are implicitly or explicitly on the christological level. Some of them are on its substance, e.g., the baptismal confession, and some of them on its form, as in the use of Greek concepts. In order to judge the dogma rightly, including the attacks upon it, one must understand its nature and significance.

Some criticisms of the christological dogma and of dogma as such, however, would not have arisen if it had been realized that dogmas do not arise for so-called "speculative" reasons. Although cognitive *eros* is not excluded from the formation of dogmas, the dogmas are, as Luther said, "protective" doctrines which are meant to preserve the substance of the Christian message against distortions from outside or inside the church. If this is understood and if the use of the dogma for political purposes is acknowledged to be a demonic distortion of its original meaning, one can, without being afraid of authoritarian consequences, attribute a positive meaning to dogma generally and to the christological dogma in particular. Then two rather different questions should be asked: To what degree did dogma succeed in reaffirming the genuine meaning of the Christian message against actual and threatening distortions? And how successful was the conceptualization of the symbols expressing the Christian message? While the first question can be answered fairly positively, the second one must be answered fairly negatively. The christological dogma saved the church, but with very inadequate conceptual tools.

The inadequacy of the tools is due partly to the inadequacy of every human concept for expressing the message of the New Being in Jesus as the Christ. It is due partly to the special inadequacy of Greek concepts, which are universally significant but nevertheless dependent upon a concrete religion determined by the divine figures of Apollo and Dionysus. Such criticism is rather different from that used by Adolf Harnack and his predecessors and followers, namely, that the use of Greek concepts by the early church inevitably led to the intellectualization of the Gospel. The assumption underlying this assertion was that Greek philosophy, in its classical as well as in its Hellenistic period, was intellectualistic by nature. But this assumption is wrong for both periods. In the archaic and classical periods, philosophy was a matter of existential importance, just as in the case of tragedy and in the mystery cults. It passionately searched—with cognitive means—for the immovable in theoretical, moral, and religious terms. Neither Socrates, Zeno, the Stoics, Plotinus, nor the Neo-Platonists can be described as being intellectualistic; and in the Hellenistic period the term "intellectualistic" sounds almost absurd. Even the philosophical schools of later antiquity were organized into cult communities, identifying the term "dogma" with their basic insights, affirming the inspired authority of their founders, and demanding acceptance of basic doctrines by their members.

Using Greek concepts does not mean intellectualizing the Christian message. More to the point is the assertion that it means the Hellenization of the Christian message. One can certainly say that the christological dogma has a Hellenistic character. But this was inescapable in the church's missionary activity in the Hellenistic world. In order to be received, the church had to use the forms of life and thought which were created by the various sources of Hellenism and which coalesced at the end of the ancient world. Three of them were of outstanding importance for the Christian church: the mystery cults, the philosophical schools, and the Roman state. Christianity adapted itself to all of them. It became a mystery cult, a philosophical school, and a legal system. But it did not cease to be an assembly based on the message that Jesus is the Christ. It remained the church in Hellenistic forms of life and thought. It did not identify itself with any of them but transformed them and even remained critical in respect to their transformation. In spite of long periods of traditionalism, the church was able to rise to moments of self-criticism and to reconsider the adapted forms.

The christological dogma uses Greek concepts, which had already undergone a Hellenizing transformation in the Hellenistic period, as in the concept of Logos. This process continued, and to it was added the Christianization of concepts. But even in this form the concepts (as, in the practical realm, the institutions) put a perpetual problem before Christian theology. For instance, in discussing the christological dogma the following questions must be asked: Does the dogmatic statement accomplish what it is supposed to, namely, to reaffirm the message of Jesus as the Christ against actual distortions and to provide a conceptually clear expression of the meaning of the message? In this respect, a dogmatic statement can fail in two possible ways. It can fail both in its substance and in its conceptual form. An example of the first failure is the half-monophysitic changes in the creed of Chalcedon since the middle of the sixth century. In this instance it was not the use of Greek philosophical concepts which caused a distortion of the original message; it was the influence on the councils of a very powerful stream of magic-superstitious piety. An example of the inadequacy of the conceptual form is the formula of Chalcedon itself. By intent and design, it was true to the genuine meaning of the Christian message. It saved Christianity from a complete elimination of the picture of Jesus as the Christ, in so far as the participation of the New Being in the state of estrangement is concerned. But it did so—and it could not have done otherwise within the conceptual frame used—through an accumulation of powerful paradoxa. It was unable to give a constructive interpretation, although this was just the reason for the original introduction of the philosophical concepts. Theology should not assign blame to its necessary conceptual tools when the failure is due to a deteriorized piety, nor should it attribute inadequacies of conceptual tools to a religious weakness. Nor should it try to get rid of all philosophical concepts. That would actually mean getting rid of itself! Theology must be free from and for the concepts it uses. It must be free from a confusion of its conceptual form with its substance, and it must be free to express this substance with every tool which proves to be more adequate than those given by the ecclesiastical tradition.

2. DANGERS AND DECISIONS IN THE DEVELOPMENT OF THE CHRISTOLOGICAL DOGMA

The two dangers which threaten every christological statement are immediate consequences of the assertion that Jesus is the Christ. The attempt to interpret this assertion conceptually can lead to an actual denial of the Christ-character of Jesus as the Christ; or it can lead to an actual denial of the Jesus-character of Jesus as the Christ. Christology must always find its way on the ridge between these two chasms, and it must know that it will never completely succeed, inasmuch as it touches the divine mystery, which remains mystery even in its manifestation.

In traditional terms the problem has been discussed as the relation of the divine to the human "nature" in Jesus. Any diminution of the human nature would deprive the Christ of his total participation in the conditions of existence. And any diminution of the divine nature would deprive the Christ of his total victory over existential estrangement. In both cases he could not have created the New Being. His being would have been less than the New Being. Therefore, the problem was how to think the unity of a completely human with a completely divine nature. This problem never has been solved adequately, even within the limits of human possibilities. The doctrine of the two natures in the Christ raises the right question but uses wrong conceptual tools. The basic inadequacy lies in the term "nature." When applied to man, it is ambiguous; when applied to God, it is wrong. This explains the inescapable definitive failure of the councils, e.g., of Nicaea and Chalcedon, in spite of their substantial truth and their historical significance.

The decision of Nicaea, defended by Athanasius as a matter of life and death for the church, made it inadmissible to deny the divine power of the Christ in revelation and salvation. In the terminology of the Nicaean controversy, the power of the Christ is the power of the divine Logos, the principle of divine self-manifestation. This leads to the question of whether the Logos is equal in divine power with the Father or less than he. If the first answer is given, the distinction between the Father and the Son seems to disappear, as in the Sabellian heresy. If the second answer is given, the Logos, even if called the greatest of all creatures, is a creature nevertheless and therefore unable to save the creation, as in the Arian heresy. Only the God who is really God can create the New Being, not a half-god. It was the term *homo-ousios,* "of equal essence," which was supposed to express this idea. But in that case, the semi-Arians asked, how could a difference exist between the Father and the Son, and does not the picture of the Jesus of history become completely ununderstandable? It was hard for Athanasius and his most intimate followers (e.g., Marcellus) to answer such questions.

The Nicaean formula has often been considered the basic Trinitarian statement of the church. It has been distinguished from the christological decisions of the fifth century, but that is misleading. The doctrine of the Trinity has independent roots in the encounter with God in all his manifestations. We have tried to show that the idea of the "living God" requires a distinction between the abysmal element of the divine, the form element, and their spiritual unity. This explains the manifold forms in which Trinitarian symbolism appears in the history of religion. The Christian doctrine of the Trinity systematizes the idea and adds the decisive element of the relation of the Christ to the Logos. It was this latter point which led to a systematically developed Trinitarian dogma. The decision of Nicaea is a christological one, although it also made the basic contribution to the Trinitarian dogma. In the same way the restatement and enlargement of Nicaea in Constantinople (381) was a christological statement, although it added the divinity of the Holy Spirit to the divinity of the Logos. If the being of Jesus as the Christ is the New Being, the human spirit of the man Jesus cannot make him into the Christ; then it must be the divine Spirit, which, like the Logos, cannot be inferior to God. Although the final discussion of the Trinitarian doctrine must await the development of the idea of the Spirit (Part IV), it can be stated here that the Trinitarian symbols become empty if they are separated from their two experiential roots—

the experience of the living God and the experience of the New Being in the Christ. Both Augustine and Luther had a feeling for this situation. Augustine found that the distinction among the three *personae* (*not* persons) in the Trinity is without any content and is used, "not in order to say something, but in order not to remain silent." And, indeed, terms like "non-generated," "eternally generated," "proceeding," even if understood as symbols—which they certainly are—do not say anything which could be meaningful for symbolic imagination. Luther found that a word like "Trinity" is strange and almost ridiculous but that here, as in other instances, there was no better one. Since he was aware of the two existential roots of the Trinitarian idea, he rejected a theology which makes the Trinitarian dialectic into a play with meaningless number combinations. The Trinitarian dogma is a supporting part of the christological dogma; and the decision of Nicaea saved Christianity from a relapse to a cult of half-gods. It rejected interpretations of Jesus as the Christ which would have deprived him of his power to create the New Being.

The decision at Nicaea that God himself and not a half-god is present in the man Jesus of Nazareth was open to the loss of the Jesus-character of Jesus as the Christ or, in traditional terminology, to the denial of his full human nature. And this danger, as we have indicated several times, was real. Popular and monastic piety was not satisfied with the message of the eternal unity of God and man appearing under the conditions of estrangement. These pieties wanted "more." They wanted a God, walking on earth, participating in history, but not involved in the conflicts of existence and the ambiguities of life. Popular piety did not want a paradox but a "miracle." It desired an event in analogy with all other events in time and space, an "objective" happening in the supranatural sense. By this kind of piety the way for every possible superstition was opened. Christianity was in danger of being swallowed up in the tidal wave of a "secondary religion," for which monophysitism provided the theological justification. This danger soon became real in countries like Egypt, which, partly for this reason, became an easy prey to iconoclastic Islam. The danger would have been more easily overcome if it had not been for the support that such popular piety found in the intensive and developing ascetic-monastic movements and their direct influence on the deciding synods. The hostility of the monks toward the natural, not only in its existential distortion, but also in its essential goodness, made them fanatical enemies of a theology which emphasized the total participation of the Christ in man's existential predicament. In the great Bishop of Alexandria, Cyril, the alliance of popular and monastic piety found a theologically cautious and politically skilful defender. The monophysitic tendency would have prevailed in the whole church in a sophisticated form if there had not been a partly victorious opposition.

The opposition came from theologians who took seriously the participation of Jesus in man's existential predicament. It also came from church leaders like Pope Leo of Rome, who, in the line of his Western tradition, emphasized the historical-dynamic character of the New Being in the Christ over against its static-hierarchical character in the East. This opposition was largely victorious in the Council of Chalcedon —in spite of the shortcomings of the Chalcedonian formula. This victory prevented the elimination of the Jesus-character of the Christ, in spite of later successful attempts in the East (Constantinople) to restate the decision of Chalcedon along the lines of Cyril. The authority of Chalcedon was too well established and the spirit of Chalcedon was too much in agreement with basic trends of Western piety—including later Protestant piety—for it to be defeated.

Chalcedon preserved Jesus

In the two great decisions of the early church, both the Christ-character and the Jesus-character of the event of Jesus as the Christ were preserved. And this happened in spite of the very inadequate conceptual tools. This is the judgment about the christological work of the church underlying the present christological exposition.

3. THE CHRISTOLOGICAL TASK OF PRESENT THEOLOGY

The general consequences which must be drawn from the preceding judgment are obvious but need concrete elaboration. Protestant theology must accept the "Catholic" tradition in so far as it is based on the substance of the two great decisions of the early church (Nicaea and Chalcedon). Protestant theology must try to find new forms in which the christological substance of the past can be expressed. The preceding christological sections are an attempt to do so. They imply a critical attitude to both the orthodox and the liberal Christologies of the last centuries of Protestant theology. The development of Protestant orthodoxy, both in its classical period and in its later reformulations, showed the impossibility of an understandable solution to the christological problem in terms of the classical terminology. It was the merit of theological liberalism that it showed through historical-critical investigations, as, e.g., in Harnack's *History of the Dogma*—the inescapable contradictions and absurdities into which all attempts to solve the christological problem in terms of the two-nature theory were driven. But liberalism itself did not contribute much to Christology in systematic terms. By saying that "Jesus does not belong within the gospel pronounced by Jesus," it eliminated the Christ-character of the event Jesus the Christ. Even historians like Albert Schweitzer, who emphasized the eschatological character of the message of Jesus and his self-interpretation as a central figure within the eschatological scheme, did not use this element for their Christology. They dismissed it as a complex of strange imagination and as a matter of apocalyptic ecstasy. The Christ-character of the event was drawn into the Jesus-character. It would be unfair, however, to identify liberal theology with Arianism. Its picture of Jesus is not that of a half-god. Rather, it is the picture of a man in whom God was manifest in a unique way. But it is not the picture of a man whose being was the New Being and who was able to conquer existential estrangement. Neither the orthodox nor the liberal methods of Protestant theology are adequate for the christological task which the Protestant church must now fulfil.

Ch

The early church was well aware that Christology is an existentially necessary, though not a theoretically interesting, work of the church. Its ultimate criterion, therefore, is existential itself. It is "soteriological," i.e., determined by the question of salvation. The greater the things we say about the Christ, the greater the salvation we can expect from him. This word of an Apostolic Father is valid for all christological thought. Differences, of course, arise if one tries to give a definition of what "great" means in relation to the Christ. For monophysitic thinking in its nuances from the early church up to today, great things are said about the Christ if his smallness, namely, his participation in finitude and tragedy, is swallowed up in his greatness, namely, his power of conquering existential estrangement. This emphasis on the "divine nature" is called a "high" Christology. But however high the divine predicates may be which are heaped on the Christ, the result is a Christology of low value, because it removes the paradox for the sake of a supranatural miracle. And salvation can be derived only from him who fully participated in man's existential predicament, not from a God

walking on earth, "unequal to us in all respects." The Protestant principle, according to which God is near to the lowest as well as to the
highest and according to which salvation is not the transference of man
from the material to a so-called spiritual world, demands a "low Christology"—which actually is the truly high Christology. By this criterion,
the preceding christological attempt should be judged.

Reference has already been made to the concept of nature used in
the terms "divine nature" and "human nature," and it has been indicated that the term "human nature" is ambiguous and the term "divine nature" is wholly inadequate. Human nature can mean man's essential or created nature; it can mean man's existential or estranged na-
ture; and it can mean man's nature in the ambiguous unity of the two
others. If we apply the term "human nature" to Jesus as the Christ, we
must say that he has a complete human nature in the first sense of the
word. Through creation, he is finite freedom, like every human being.
With respect to the second meaning of "human nature," we must say
that he has man's existential nature as a real possibility, but in such a
way that temptation, which is the possibility, is always taken into the
unity with God. From this it follows that, in the third sense, human
nature must be attributed to Jesus in so far as he is involved in the tragic
ambiguities of life. Under these circumstances it is imperative to dismiss
altogether the term "human nature" in relation to the Christ and replace it by a description of the dynamics of his life—as we have tried
to do.

In a culture in which nature was the all-embracing concept, the term
"human nature" was adequate. Men, gods, and all other beings which
constitute the universe belong to nature, to that which grows by itself.
If God is understood as he who transcends everything created, qualitatively and infinitely, the term "divine nature" can mean only that which
makes God into God, that which one must think if one thinks of God.
In this sense, nature is essence. But God has no essence separated from
existence, he is beyond essence and existence. He is what he is, eternally by himself. This could also be called God's essential nature. But
then one actually says that it is essential for God that he transcend
every essence. A more concrete symbolic expression of this idea is that
God is eternally creative, that through himself he creates the world and
through the world himself. There is no divine nature which could be
abstracted from his eternal creativity.

This analysis discloses that the term "divine nature" is questionable and that it cannot be applied to the Christ in any meaningful way; for the Christ (who is Jesus of Nazareth) is not beyond essence and existence. If he were, he could not be a personal life living in a limited period of time, having been born and having to die, being finite, tempted, and tragically involved in existence. The assertion that Jesus as the Christ is the personal unity of a divine and a human nature must be replaced by the assertion that in Jesus as the Christ the eternal unity of God and man has become historical reality. In his being, the New Being is real, and the New Being is the re-established unity between God and man. We replace the inadequate concept "divine nature" by the concepts "eternal God-man-unity" or "Eternal God-Manhood." Such concepts replace a static essence by a dynamic relation. The uniqueness of this relation is in no way reduced by its dynamic character; but, by eliminating the concept of "two natures," which lie beside each other like blocks and whose unity cannot be understood at all, we are open to relational concepts which make understandable the dynamic picture of Jesus as the Christ.

In both of these terms the word "eternal" is added to the relational description. "Eternal" points to the general presupposition of the unique event Jesus as the Christ. This event could not have taken place if there had not been an eternal unity of God and man within the divine life. This unity in a state of pure essentiality or potentiality can become actualized through finite freedom and, in the unique event Jesus as the Christ, became actualized against existential disruption. The character of this unity has been described in the concrete terms of the Gospel stories. Abstract definitions of the nature of this unity are as impossible as psychological investigations into its character. One can only say that it is a community between God and the center of a personal life which determines all utterances of this life and resists the attempts within existential estrangement to disrupt it.

The question now arises as to whether the replacement of the two-nature theory by dynamic-relational concepts does not remove the important idea of "Incarnation." Is not a relational concept a return from a Christology of Incarnation to a Christology of adoption? First of all, one can answer that both the incarnational and the adoptionist Christologies have biblical roots and, for this and other reasons, a genuine standing in Christian thought. But, beyond this, one must say that neither of them can be carried out without the other. Adoptionism, the idea that God through his Spirit adopted the man Jesus as his Messiah, leads to the question: Why just him? And this question leads back to the polarity of freedom and destiny which created the uninterrupted unity between him and God. The story of the virgin birth traces this unity back to his very beginning and even beyond it to his ancestors. The symbol of his pre-existence gives the eternal dimension, and the doctrine of the Logos, which became historical reality (flesh), points to what has been called "Incarnation." The incarnational Christology was needed to explain the adoptionist Christology. This was a necessary development. But it is equally necessary—although not always seen—that incarnational Christology needs adoptionist Christology for its fulfilment. The term "Incarnation" in itself is adequate (like the term "divine nature") in paganism. Since the gods belong to the universe, they can easily enter all forms of the universe; endless metamorphoses are possible. When Christianity uses the term "Incarnation," it tries to express the paradox that he who transcends the universe appears in it and under its conditions. In this sense every Christology is an incarnational Christology. But the connotation of the term leads to ideas which can hardly be distinguished from pagan transmutation myths. If the *egeneto* in the Johannine sentence, *Logos sarx egeneto,* the "Word became flesh," is pressed, we are in the midst of a mythology of metamorphosis. And it is natural that the question should arise concerning how something which *becomes* something else can remain at the same time what it is. Or did the Logos otherwise disappear when Jesus of Nazareth was born? Here absurdity replaces thought, and faith is called the acceptance of absurdities. The Incarnation of the Logos is not metamorphosis but his total manifestation in a personal life. But manifestation in a personal life is a dynamic process involving tensions, risks, dangers, and determination by freedom as well as by destiny. This is the adoption side, without which the Incarnation accent would make unreal the living picture of the Christ. He would be deprived of his finite freedom; for a transmuted divine being does not have the freedom to be other than divine. He would be without serious temptation. Protestantism favors the given solution. It does not deny the idea of Incarnation, but it removes the pagan connotations and rejects its supranaturalistic interpretation. As Protestantism asserts the justification of the sinner, so it demands a Christology of the participation of the Christ in sinful existence, including, at the same time, its conquest. The christological paradox and the paradox of the justification of the sinner are one and the same paradox. It is the paradox of God accepting a world which rejects him.

Some traits of the christological position taken here are similar to Schleiermacher's Christology, as developed in his *Glaubenslehre*. He replaces the two-nature doctrine by a doctrine of a divine-human relation. He speaks of a God-consciousness in Jesus, the strength of which surpasses the God-consciousness of all other men. He describes Jesus as the *Urbild* ("original image") of what man essentially is and from which he has fallen. The similarity is obvious; but it is not identity. Essential God-Manhood points to both sides of the relation and this in terms of eternity. It is an objective structure and not a state of man. The phrase "essential unity between God and man" has an ontological character; Schleiermacher's God-consciousness has an anthropological character. The term *Urbild* when used for Jesus as the Christ does not have the decisive implication of the term "New Being." In *Urbild* the idealistic transcendence of true humanity over human existence is clearly expressed, while in "New Being," the participation of him who is *also* the *Urbild* ("essential man") is decisive. The New Being is new not only over against existence but also over against essence, in so far as essence remains mere potentiality. The *Urbild* remains unmoved above existence; the New Being participates in existence and conquers it. Here again an ontological element makes the difference. But these differences, expressing variant presuppositions and consequences, should not hide the fact that similar problems and solutions arise when Protestant theology takes a path lying between classical and liberal Christology. This is our present situation. In the problems it puts before us, we must seek for solutions.

D. THE UNIVERSAL SIGNIFICANCE OF THE EVENT JESUS THE CHRIST

1. The Uniqueness and the Universality of the Event

Christology is a function of soteriology. The problem of soteriology creates the christological question and gives direction to the christological answer. For it is the Christ who brings the New Being, who saves men from the old being, that is, from existential estrangement and its self-destructive consequences. This criterion has been presupposed in all the christological assertions, but we must now consider it directly. We must ask in what sense and in what way Jesus as the Christ is the savior or, more precisely, in what way the unique event of Jesus as the Christ has universal significance for every human being and, indirectly, for the universe as well.

The biblical picture of Jesus is that of a unique event. Jesus appears as an individual beside others, but unique in his destiny, in every single trait of his character, and in his historical setting. It was just this concreteness and incomparable uniqueness of the "real" picture which gave Christianity its superiority over mystery cults and Gnostic visions. A real, individual life shines through all his utterances and actions. In comparison, the divine figures of the mystery cults remain abstract, without the fresh colors of a life really lived and without historical destiny and the tensions of finite freedom. The picture of Jesus as the Christ conquered them through the power of a concrete reality.

Nevertheless, the New Testament was not interested in telling the story of a uniquely interesting man. It intended to give the picture of the one who is the Christ and who, for this reason, has universal significance. At the same time, the New Testament does not erase the individual traits in the picture of the Christ but relates them rather to his character as the Christ. Every trait in the New Testament records becomes translucent for the New Being, which is his being. In every expression of his individuality appears his universal significance.

We have distinguished between historical, legendary, and mythical elements in the biblical records. For the purpose of showing the universality of Jesus as the Christ within his individuality, this distinction provides three ways of looking at the biblical materials. The one way is that of historical reports which were chosen according to their value in answering the questions of human existence generally and of the early congregations especially. This produces what has been called the "anecdotal" character of the Gospel stories. The second way emphasizes the universal quality of particular stories through a more or less legendary form. The third way expresses the universal meaning of the whole event of Jesus of Nazareth in symbols and myths. The three ways often overlap, but the third way is decisive for christological thought. The latter has the character of a direct confession and thereby provides the materials for the creedal expressions of the Christian faith. In order to describe the universal significance of Jesus as the Christ on the basis of the biblical literature, one must hold to the symbols and use the historical and legendary stories only in a corroborative sense.

But symbols and myths raise a problem which has come to the fore in the discussion about the "demythologization" of the New Testament. Although there are some "dated" features in the discussion, it has significance for the whole of Christian history and for the history of religion generally. In our earlier treatment of the nature of historical research and of the reception of the Christ, the basic point was that christological symbols are the way in which the historical fact, called Jesus of Nazareth, has been received by those who consider him to be the Christ. These symbols must be understood as symbols, and they lose their meaning if taken literally. In dealing with the christological symbols, we were engaged not in a "demythologization" but in a "deliteralization." We tried to affirm and to intercept them as symbols. "Demythologization" can mean two things, and the failure to distinguish between them has led to the confusion which characterizes the discussion. It can mean the fight against the literalistic distortion of symbols and myths. This is a necessary task of Christian theology. It keeps Christianity from falling into a wave of superstitious "objectivations" of the holy. But demythologization can also mean the removal of myth as a vehicle of religious expression and the substitution of science and morals. In this sense demythologization must be strongly rejected. It would deprive religion of its language; it would silence the experience of the holy. Symbols and myths cannot be criticized simply because they are symbols. They must be criticized on the basis of their power to express what they are supposed to express, namely, in this instance, the New Being in Jesus as the Christ.

This is the attitude for approaching those symbols and myths in which the universal meaning of Jesus as the Christ is expressed. Each of these symbols shows him as the bearer of the New Being in a special relation to existence. For systematic reasons, anticipated in the New Testament, one can single out two central symbols. These correspond to the two basic relations of the Christ to existential estrangement, and they have determined the development of and the conflicts about the christological dogma. The first relation of the Christ to existence is his subjection to it; the second relation of the Christ to existence is his conquest of it. All other relations are directly or indirectly dependent on these two. Each of them is expressed by a central symbol. The subjection to existence is expressed in the symbol of the "Cross of the Christ"; the conquest of existence is expressed in the symbol of the "Resurrection of the Christ."

2. The Central Symbols of the Universal Significance of Jesus as the Christ and Their Relation

The "Cross of the Christ" and the "Resurrection of the Christ" are interdependent symbols; they cannot be separated without losing their meaning. The Cross of the Christ is the Cross of the one who has conquered the death of existential estrangement. Otherwise it would only be one more tragic event (which it *also* is) in the long history of the tragedy of man. And the Resurrection of the Christ is the Resurrection of the one who, as the Christ, subjected himself to the death of existential estrangement. Otherwise it would be only one more questionable miracle story (which it also is in the records).

If Cross and Resurrection are interdependent, they must be both reality and symbol. In both cases something happened within existence. Otherwise the Christ would not have entered existence and could not have conquered it. But there is a qualitative difference. While the stories of the Cross probably point to an event that took place in the full light of historical observation, the stories of the Resurrection spread a veil of deep mystery over the event. The one is a highly probable fact; the other a mysterious experience of a few. One can ask whether this qualitative difference does not make a real interdependence impossible? Is it perhaps wiser to follow the suggestion of those scholars who understand the Resurrection as a symbolic interpretation of the Cross without any kind of objective reality?

The New Testament lays tremendous significance on the objective side of the Resurrection; at the same time, it elevates the objective event indicated in the stories of the Crucifixion to universal symbolic significance. One could say that in the minds of the disciples and of the writers of the New Testament the Cross is both an event and a symbol and that the Resurrection is both a symbol and an event. Certainly, the Cross of Jesus is seen as an event that happened in time and space. But, as the Cross of the Jesus who is the Christ, it is a symbol and a part of a myth. It is the myth of the bearer of the new eon who suffers the death of a convict and slave under the powers of that old eon which he is to conquer. This Cross, whatever the historical circumstances may have been, is a symbol based on a fact.

But the same is true of the Resurrection. The resurrection of gods and half-gods is a familiar mythological symbol. It plays a major role in some mystery cults in which mystical participation in the death and the resurrection of the god on the part of the initiated is the ritual center. A belief in the future resurrection of the martyrs grew up in later Judaism. In the moment in which Jesus was called the Christ and the combination of his messianic dignity with an ignominious death was asserted—whether in expectation or in retrospection—the application of the idea of resurrection to the Christ was almost unavoidable. The disciples' assertion that the symbol had become an event was dependent in part upon their belief in Jesus, who, as the Christ, became the Messiah. But it was affirmed in a way which transcended the mythological symbolism of the mystery cults, just as the concrete picture of Jesus as the Christ transcended the mythical pictures of the mystery gods. The character of this event remains in darkness, even in the poetic rationalization of the Easter story. But one thing is obvious. In the days in which the certainty of his Resurrection grasped the small, dispersed, and despairing group of his followers, the church was born, and, since the Christ is not the Christ without the church, he has become the Christ. The certainty that he who is the bringer of the new eon cannot finally have succumbed to the powers of the old eon made the experience of the Resurrection the decisive test of the Christ-character of Jesus of Nazareth. A real experience made it possible for the disciples to apply the known symbol of resurrection to Jesus, thus acknowledging him definitely as the Christ. They called this experienced event the "Resurrection of the Christ," and it was a combination of event and symbol.

The attempt has been made to describe both events, the Cross and the Resurrection, as factual events separated from their symbolic meaning. This is justified, in so far as the significance of both symbols rests on the combination of symbol and fact. Without the factual element, the Christ would not have participated in existence and consequently not have been the Christ. But the desire to isolate the factual from the symbolic element is, as has been shown before, not a primary interest of faith. The results of the research for the purely factual element can never be on the basis of faith or theology.

With this in mind, one can say that the historical event underlying the Crucifixion story shines with comparative clarity through the different and often contradictory legendary reports. Those who regard the passion story as cult-legend, which is told in various ways, simply agree with the thesis presented about the symbolic character of the Cross of the Jesus who is the Christ. The only factual element in it having the immediate certainty of faith is the surrender of him who is called the Christ to the ultimate consequence of existence, namely, death under the conditions of estrangement. Everything else is a matter of historical probability, elaborated out of legendary interpretation.

The event which underlies the symbol of the Resurrection must be treated in an analogous way. The factual element is a necessary implication of the symbol of the Resurrection (as it is of the symbol of the Cross). Historical research is justified in trying to elaborate this factual element on the basis of the legendary and mythological material which surrounds it. But historical research can never give more than a probable answer. The faith in the Resurrection of the Christ is neither positively nor negatively dependent on it. Faith can give certainty only to the victory of the Christ over the ultimate consequence of the existential estrangement to which he subjected himself. And faith can give this certainty because it is itself based on it. Faith is based on the experience of being grasped by the power of the New Being through which the destructive consequences of estrangement are conquered.

It is the certainty of one's own victory over the death of existential estrangement which creates the certainty of the Resurrection of the Christ as event and symbol; but it is not historical conviction or the acceptance of biblical authority which creates this certainty. Beyond this point there is no certainty but only probability, often very low, sometimes rather high.

There are three theories which try to make the event of the Resurrection probable. The most primitive theory, and at the same time most beautifully expressed, is the physical one. It is told in the story of the tomb which the women found empty on Easter morning. The sources of this story are rather late and questionable, and there is no indication of it in the earliest tradition concerning the event of the Resurrection, namely I Corinthians, chapter 15. Theologically speaking, it is a rationalization of the event, interpreting it with physical categories that identify resurrection with the presence or absence of a physical body. Then the absurd question arises as to what happened to the molecules which comprise the corpse of Jesus of Nazareth. Then absurdity becomes compounded into blasphemy.

A second attempt to penetrate into the factual side of the Resurrection event is the spiritualistic one. It uses, above all, the appearances of the Resurrected as recorded by Paul. It explains them as manifestations of the soul of the man Jesus to his followers, in analogy to the self-manifestations of the souls of the dead in spiritualistic experiences. Obviously, this is not the Resurrection of the Christ but an attempt to prove the general immortality of the soul and the claim that it has the general ability after death to manifest itself to the living. Spiritualistic experiences may or may not be valid. But, even if valid, they cannot explain the factual side of the Resurrection of the Christ symbolized as the reappearance of the total personality, which includes the bodily expression of his being. This is so much the case that he can be recognized in a way which is more than the manifestation of a bodiless "spirit."

The third attempt to approach the factual side of the Resurrection is the psychological one. It is the easiest and most accepted way of describing the factual element in the Resurrection. Resurrection is an inner event in the minds of Jesus' adherents. Paul's description of the Resurrection experiences (including his own) lends itself to the psychological interpretation. And—if we exclude the physical interpretation—Paul's words, like the story of his conversion, point to something which happened in the minds of those who had the experiences. This does not imply that the event itself was "merely" psychological, namely, wholly dependent on psychological factors in the minds of those whom Paul enumerates (e.g., an intensification of the memory of Jesus). But the psychological theory misses the reality of the event which is presupposed in the symbol—the event of the Resurrection of the Christ.

We must ask anew what this reality is? In order to describe it, we must look at the negativity which is overcome in it. Certainly, it is not the death of an individual man, no matter how important. Therefore, the revival of an individual man or his reappearance as a spirit cannot be the event of Resurrection. The negativity which is overcome in the Resurrection is that of the disappearance of him whose being was the New Being. It is the overcoming of his disappearance from present experience and his consequent transition into the past except for the limits

of memory. And, since the conquest of such transitoriness is essential
for the New Being, Jesus, it appeared, could not have been its bearer.
At the same time, the power of his being had impressed itself indelibly
upon the disciples as the power of the New Being. In this tension something unique happened. In an ecstatic experience the concrete picture
of Jesus of Nazareth became indissolubly united with the reality of the
New Being. He is present wherever the New Being is present. Death
was not able to push him into the past. But this presence does not have
the character of a revived (and transmuted) body, nor does it have the
character of the reappearance of an individual soul; it has the character
of spiritual presence. He "is the Spirit" and we "know him now" only
because he is the Spirit. In this way the concrete individual life of the
man Jesus of Nazareth is raised above transitoriness into the eternal
presence of God as Spirit. This event happened first to some of his followers who had fled to Galilee in the hours of his execution; then to
many others; then to Paul; then to all those who in every period experience his living presence here and now. This is the event. It has been
interpreted through the symbol "Resurrection" which was readily available in the thought forms of that day. The combination of symbol and
event is the central Christian symbol, the Resurrection of the Christ.

The preceding theory concerning the event which underlies the sym-
bol of Resurrection dismisses physical as well as spiritualistic literalism.
It replaces both by a description which keeps nearer to the oldest source
(I Cor., chap. 15) and which places at the center of its analysis the
religious meaning of the Resurrection for the disciples (and all their
followers), in contrast to their previous state of negativity and despair.
This view is the ecstatic confirmation of the indestructible unity of the
New Being and its bearer, Jesus of Nazareth. In eternity they belong
together. In contrast to the physical, the spiritualistic, and the psychological theories concerning the Resurrection event, one could call this
the "restitution theory." According to it, the Resurrection is the restitution of Jesus as the Christ, a restitution which is rooted in the personal
unity between Jesus and God and in the impact of this unity on the
minds of the apostles. Historically, it may well be that the restitution
of Jesus to the dignity of the Christ in the minds of the disciples may
precede the story of the acceptance of Jesus as the Christ by Peter. The
latter may be a reflex of the former; but, even if this is the case, the

experience of the New Being in Jesus must precede the experience of the Resurrected.

Although it is my conviction that the restitution theory is most adequate to the facts, it must also be considered a theory. It remains in the realm of probability and does not have the certainty of faith. Faith provides the certainty that the picture of the Christ in the Gospels is a personal life in which the New Being has appeared in its fulness and that the death of Jesus of Nazareth was not able to separate the New Being from the picture of its bearer. If physical or spiritualistic literalists are not satisfied with this solution, they cannot be forced to accept it in the name of faith. But they can perhaps grant that the attitude of the New Testament and especially of the non-literalistic Apostle Paul justifies the theory of restitution.

3. Symbols Corroborating the Symbol "Cross of the Christ"

The story of the Cross of Jesus as the Christ does not report an isolated event in his life but that event toward which the story of his life is directed and in which the others receive their meaning. Their meaning is that he who is the Christ subjects himself to the ultimate negativities of existence and that they are not able to separate him from his unity with God. Thus we find other symbols in the New Testament which point to and corroborate the more central symbol of the Cross of Jesus as the Christ.

The idea of the subjection of the self is expressed by Paul in mythical terms in Philippians, chapter 2. The pre-existent Christ gave up his divine form, became a servant, and experienced the death of a slave. Pre-existence and self-surrender are combined in this symbolism. It corroborates the central symbol of the Cross, but it cannot be taken literally as an event which happened at some time in some heavenly place. The same idea is expressed in legendary terms in the stories of the birth of Christ in Bethlehem, his lying in a cradle, his flight to Egypt, and the early threat to his life by the political powers.

Also preparing for and corroborating the symbolic meaning of the Cross are the descriptions of his subjection to finitude and its categories. In many of the descriptions, which include the tension between his messianic dignity and the low conditions of his existence, the character of "subjection" to existence is indicated. In the scene of Gethsemane, of his death and burial, all this comes to a climax. All these traits, which could easily be multiplied and elaborated, are summed up in the symbol of the Cross. The Cross should not be separated from them, just as they should be interpreted in their totality as expressions of the subjection of him in whom the New Being is present to the conditions of existential estrangement. Whether these expressions are mythical, legendary, historical, or mixtures of all of them, they as well as the Cross, for which they are supporting symbols, are not important in themselves in the context of the biblical picture. They are important in their power to show the subjection of him who is the bearer of the New Being to the destructive structures of the old being. They are symbols of the divine paradox of the appearance of the eternal God-man unity within existential estrangement. One of the great features of the Apostles' Creed is that in the all-embracing second article it has enumerated symbols of subjection along with the symbols of victory. In doing so, it anticipated the basic structure in which the universal significance of Jesus the Christ as the bearer of the New Being must be seen.

4. Symbols Corroborating the Symbol "Resurrection of the Christ"

Like the story of the Cross, the story of the Resurrection of the Christ does not report an isolated event after his death. It reports the event which is anticipated in a large number of other events and which is, at the same time, their confirmation. The Resurrection, as well as the historical, legendary, and mythological symbols corroborating it, show the New Being in Jesus as the Christ as victorious over the existential estrangement to which he has subjected himself. This is their universal significance.

As in the discussion of the symbols of subjection, we must start with the mythical symbol of pre-existence and add to it that of postexistence. While pre-existence in connection with the symbols of subjection was the precondition for the transcendent self-humiliation of the Christ, it must be considered in the present context in its own significance and as a corroborating symbol for the Resurrection. It expresses the eternal root of the New Being as it is historically present in the event Jesus the Christ. When, according to the Fourth Gospel, Jesus says that he precedes Abraham, this is a kind of preceding that cannot be understood horizontally (as the Jews in the story could not help doing) but vertically. This is also an implication of the Logos doctrine of the Fourth Gospel and points to the presence of the eternal principle of the divine self-manifestation in Jesus of Nazareth.

The symbol of postexistence corresponds to the symbol of pre-existence. It also lies in the vertical dimension not as the eternal presupposition of the historical appearance of the New Being in Jesus as the Christ but as its eternal confirmation. The special symbols, connected with postexistence, will be discussed presently. At this point it seems necessary to warn against a literalism which takes pre-existence and postexistence as stages in a transcendent story of a divine being which descends from and ascends to a heavenly place. Descending and ascending are spatial metaphors indicating the eternal dimension in the subjection of the bearer of the New Being to existence and in the victory of the bearer of the New Being over existence.

While the birth of Jesus in Bethlehem belongs to the symbols corroborating the Cross, the story of the virgin birth belongs to the symbols corroborating the Resurrection. It expresses the conviction that the divine Spirit who has made the man Jesus of Nazareth into the Messiah has already created him as his vessel, so that the saving appearance of the New Being is independent of historical contingencies and dependent on God alone. It is the same motif which led to the Logos Christology, even though it belongs to another line of thought. The factual element in it is that historical destiny determined the bearer of the New Being, even before his birth. But the actual story is a myth, the symbolic value of which must be seriously questioned. It points toward the docetic-monophysitic direction of Christian thinking and is itself an important step in it. By excluding the participation of a human father in the procreation of the Messiah, it deprives him of full participation in the human predicament.

A symbolically clear anticipation of the Resurrection is the story of the transfiguration of Jesus and his conversation with Moses and Elijah.

The biblical records are full of miracle stories, and some of them are significant in pointing to the appearance of the new state of things. When the disciples of John the Baptist ask him about his messianic character, Jesus points to them as witnessing the coming of the new eon. In all the miracles performed by Jesus, some of the evils of existential self-destruction are conquered. They are not finally conquered, for the people to whom miracles happened were again subject to sickness and death and to the vicissitudes of nature. But what happened to them was a representative anticipation of the victory of the New Being over existential self-destruction. This was evident in mental and bodily sickness, in catastrophe and in want, in despair and in meaningless death.

The miracles of Jesus would not have had this function, had he done them for the sake of showing his messianic power. That approach was considered by him to be a demonic temptation coming both from his enemies and from Satan. Miracles are performed by him because he fully participates in the misery of the human situation and tries to overcome it wherever the occasion offers itself. In a special way the healing stories show the superiority of the New Being in him over mental possession and its bodily consequences. He appears as the victor over the demons, over the supra-individual structures of destruction. This point was taken up by Paul and the early church. The saving power of the New Being is, above all, power over the enslaving structures of evil. In later periods Christian teaching and preaching often neglected this basic meaning of the miracle stories and instead emphasized their miraculous character. This is one of the unfortunate consequences of the supranaturalistic frame of reference in which traditional theology saw the relation between God and the world. God's presence and power should not be sought in the supranatural interference in the ordinary course of events but in the power of the New Being to overcome the self-destructive consequences of existential estrangement in and through the created structures of reality. If taken in this sense, the miracles of Jesus as the Christ belong to the symbols of victory and corroborate the central symbol of Resurrection.

The concept of miracles in general was discussed in Part I and cannot be repeated here. Here it can only be reported that miracles are described as an ecstatically received understanding of constellations of factors which point to the divine Ground of Being. This definition was formulated on the basis of the New Testament miracle stories and the judgment about them in the New Testament itself. It is understandable, however, that legendary and mythical elements easily entered into the reports about genuinely experienced miracles. It is even more understandable that, as early as the New Testament, a rationalization took place which expressed itself in the desire to emphasize the antinatural element in the stories instead of their power to point to the presence of the divine power overcoming existential destruction.

We must now consider a consistent group of symbols, taken from the rich field of eschatological symbolism, which corroborate the Resurrection from the point of view of its consequences for the Christ, his church, and his world. These start with the symbol of the Ascension of the Christ. In some ways this is a reduplication of the Resurrection but is distinguished from it because it has a finality which contrasts markedly with the repeated experiences of the Resurrected. The finality of his separation from historical existence, indicated in the Ascension, is identical with his spiritual presence as the power of the New Being but with the concreteness of his personal countenance. It is therefore another symbolic expression of the same event which the Resurrection expresses. If taken literally, its spatial symbolism would become absurd.

The same is true of the symbol of Christ "sitting at the right hand of God." If taken literally, it is absurd and ridiculous, as Luther already felt when he identified the right hand of God with his omnipotence, that is, his power of working everything in everything. The symbol then means that God's creativity is not separated from the New Being in Christ but that in its three forms (original, preserving, directing creativity) its final aim is the actualization of the New Being as manifest in the Christ.

Immediately connected with the participation of the New Being in divine creativity is the symbol of his rule over the church through the Spirit. In fact, the church takes the criteria of his working in the church from him, namely, from the being of Jesus as the Christ which is the New Being. Another, but intimately connected, expression of the participation of the New Being in divine creativity is the symbol of him as the ruler of history. He who is the Christ and has brought the new eon is the ruler of the new eon. History is the creation of the new in every moment. But the ultimately new toward which history moves is the New Being; it is the end of history, namely, the end of the preparatory period of history and its aim. If one asks what the event is behind the symbol of the ruling of history in the Christ, the answer can only be that through historical providence the New Being is actualized in history and through history (fragmentarily and under the ambiguities of life), though under the criterion of the being of Jesus as the Christ. The symbol of the Christ as Lord of history means neither external interference by a heavenly being nor fulfilment of the New Being in history or its transformation into the Kingdom of God; but it does mean the certainty that nothing can happen in history which would make the work of the New Being impossible.

The more directly eschatological symbols must also be evaluated. One of them, the expectation of a coming period symbolized as a period of a thousand years, is much neglected in traditional theology. This is

partly because it had no prominent place in biblical literature. It is neglected partly because it had been a matter of sharp controversy since
the time of the Montanist revolt against ecclesiastical conservatism. It
was present still as a problem in the revolt of the radical Franciscans.
But it must be taken seriously in theology, because it is decisive for
the Christian interpretation of history. In contrast to a final catastrophe
in the sense of the apocalyptic visions, the symbol of the thousand
years' reign of the Christ continues the prophetic tradition in which
an inner-historical fulfilment of history is envisaged. Of course, the
symbol does not stand for a complete fulfilment. The demonic power
is banned but not eradicated, and it will return. In less mythological
language, one could say that the demonic can positively be conquered
in a special place and in a special time but not totally and universally.
The expectation of the thousand-year reign produced many utopian
movements, but it actually has in it a genuine warning against utopianism. The demonic is subdued for a time, but it is not dead!

The symbol of the "Second Coming" or the *parousia* of the Christ
has two functions. First, it expresses in a special way that Jesus is the
Christ, namely, he who cannot be transcended by anyone else who may
appear in the course of human history. Although this is clearly implicit
in the christological assertion, it must be emphasized especially for
those who speak of new superior religious experiences which might
occur and who therefore think that one must keep the future open,
even in relation to Jesus as the Christ. This problem was well known
to the author of the Fourth Gospel. He does not deny the continuation
of religious experience after the Resurrection of the Christ. He has the
Christ say that the Spirit will guide them into all truth. But he immediately warns that what the Spirit shows does not come from the
Spirit but from the Christ, who himself has nothing from himself but
everything from his Father. The one function of the symbol of the
Second Coming of the Christ is to exclude the expectation of a superior manifestation of the New Being.

But this is only one function of the symbol "Second Coming." The
other is to give an answer to the Jewish criticism that Jesus could not
have been the Messiah, since the new eon has not come and the old
state of things remains unchanged. Therefore, the Jewish argument is
that we still must wait for the coming of the Messiah. Christianity
agrees that we are in a period of waiting. It proves that, with the

increase of the power of the Kingdom of God, the demonic realm also becomes stronger and more destructive. But, in contrast to Judaism, Christianity asserts that the might of the demonic is broken in principle (in power and beginning) because the Christ has appeared in Jesus of Nazareth, the bearer of the New Being. His being is the New Being. And the New Being, the conquest of the old eon, is in those who participate in him and in the church in so far as it is based on him as its foundation. The symbol of the Second Coming of the Christ corroborates the Resurrection by placing the Christian in a period between the *kairoi,* the times in which the eternal breaks into the temporal, between an "already" and a "not yet," and subjects him to the infinite tensions of this situation in personal and in historical existence.

The ultimate judgment of the world by Christ is one of the most dramatic symbols. It has inspired artists and poets in all generations and has produced profound and often neurotic anxiety in the conscious as well as the unconscious spheres of believers. It has—as Luther tells of his own early experience—corrupted the image of the Christ as healer and savior into the image of a pitiless judge from whom one must flee under the protection of saints, analysts, or skeptics. It is important to realize that in this case the New Testament itself has started to "deliteralize" (as one should say, instead of "demythologize"). The Fourth Gospel does not deny the mythical symbol of the Last Judgment; but it describes the factual side as the crisis which happens to people who encounter the New Being and either accept it or reject it. It is an immanent judgment which is always going on in history, even where the name of Jesus is not known but where the power of the New Being, which is his being, is present or absent (Matthew, chapter 25). This immanent judgment, since it is going on under the conditions of existence, is subject to the ambiguities of life and therefore demands a symbol of an ultimate separation of the ambiguous elements of reality or their purification and elevation into the transcendent unity of the Kingdom of God.

This completes our discussion of the symbols which corroborate the central one of the Resurrection of the Christ. The symbols have been greatly distorted and consequently were rejected by many because of a literalism which makes them absurd and non-existential. Their power must be re-established by a reinterpretation which unites cosmic and existential qualities and makes it evident that a symbol is based on things and events and participates in the power of that which it symbolizes. Therefore, symbols cannot be replaced at will; they must be interpreted as long as they are alive. They may die, and some of the symbols interpreted in the preceding chapters may already be dead. For a long time they have been under justifiable and unjustifiable attacks. The theologian cannot give a judgment concerning the life or death of the symbols he interprets. This judgment occurs in the consciousness of the living church and has deep roots in the collective unconscious. It happens in the liturgical realm, in personal devotion, in preaching and in teaching, in the activities of the church toward the world, and in the quiet contemplation of its members. It happens as historical destiny and therefore ultimately through the divine creativity as united with the power of the New Being in the Christ. The New Being is not dependent on the special symbols in which it is expressed. It has the power to be free from every form in which it appears.

E. THE NEW BEING IN JESUS AS THE CHRIST AS THE POWER OF SALVATION

1. THE MEANING OF SALVATION

The universal significance of Jesus as the Christ, which is expressed in the symbols of subjection to existence and of victory over existence, can also be expressed in the term "salvation." He himself is called the Savior, the Mediator, or the Redeemer. Each of these terms demands semantic and theological clarification.

The term "salvation" has as many connotations as there are negativities from which salvation is needed. But one can distinguish salvation from ultimate negativity and from that which leads to ultimate negativity. Ultimate negativity is called condemnation or eternal death, the loss of the inner *telos* of one's being, the exclusion from the universal unity of the Kingdom of God, and the exclusion from eternal life. In the overwhelming majority of occasions in which the word "salvation" or the phrase "being saved" is used, it refers to salvation from this ultimate negativity. The tremendous weight of the question of salvation is rooted in this understanding of the term. It becomes the question of "to be or not to be."

The way in which the ultimate aim—eternal life—can be gained or lost decides about the more limited meaning of "salvation." Therefore, for the early Greek church death and error were the things from which one needed and wanted to be saved. In the Roman Catholic church salvation is from guilt and its consequences in this and the next life (in purgatory and hell). In classical Protestantism salvation is from the law, its anxiety-producing and its condemning power. In pietism and revivalism salvation is the conquest of the godless state through conversion and transformation for those who are converted. In ascetic and liberal Protestantism salvation is the conquest of special sins and progress toward moral perfection. The question of life and death in the ultimate sense has not disappeared in the latter groups (except in some forms of so-called theological humanism), but it has been pushed into the background.

With respect to both the original meaning of salvation (from *salvus,* "healed") and our present situation, it may be adequate to interpret salvation as "healing." It corresponds to the state of estrangement as the main characteristic of existence. In this sense, healing means reuniting that which is estranged, giving a center to what is split, overcoming the split between God and man, man and his world, man and himself. Out of this interpretation of salvation, the concept of the New Being has grown. Salvation is reclaiming from the old and transferring into the New Being. This understanding includes the elements of salvation which were emphasized in other periods; it includes, above all, the fulfilment of the ultimate meaning of one's existence, but it sees this in a special perspective, that of making *salvus,* of "healing."

If Christianity derives salvation from the appearance of Jesus as the Christ, it does not separate salvation through the Christ from the processes of salvation, i.e., of healing, which occur throughout all history. We have discussed the problem of "healing" universally in the section on revelation. There is a history of concrete revelatory events in all periods in which man exists as man. It would be wrong to call that history itself the history of revelation (with some theological humanists). But it would be equally wrong to deny that revelatory events occur anywhere besides the appearance of Jesus as the Christ. There is a history of revelation, the center of which is the event Jesus the Christ; but the center is not without a line which leads to it (preparatory revelation) and a line which leads from it (receiving revelation). Further, we have asserted that where there is revelation, there is salvation. Revelation is not information about divine things; it is the ecstatic manifestation of the Ground of Being in events, persons, and things. Such manifestations have shaking, transforming, and healing power. They are saving events in which the power of the New Being is present. It is present in a preparatory way, fragmentarily, and is open to demonic distortion. But it is present and heals where it is seriously accepted. On these healing forces the life of mankind always depends; they prevent the self-destructive structures of existence from plunging mankind into complete annihilation. This is true of individuals as well as of groups and is the basis for a positive evolution of the religions and cultures of mankind. However, the idea of a universal history of salvation can be developed fully only in the parts of *Systematic Theology* which deal with "Life and the Spirit" and with "History and the Kingdom of God" (Vol. III).

This view of the history of salvation excludes an unbiblical but nevertheless ecclesiastical view of salvation. It is the belief that salvation is either total or non-existent. Total salvation, in this view, is identical with being taken into the state of ultimate blessedness and is the opposite of total condemnation to everlasting pain or eternal death. If, then, the salvation to eternal life is made dependent upon the encounter with Jesus as the Christ and the acceptance of his saving power, only a small number of human beings will ever reach salvation. The others, either through a divine decree or through the destiny which came upon them from Adam's Fall or through their own guilt, are condemned to exclusion from eternal life. Theologies of universalism always tried to escape this absurd and demonic idea, but it is difficult to do so, once the absolute alternative between salvation and condemnation is presupposed. Only if salvation is understood as healing and saving power through the New Being in all history is the problem put on another level. In some degree all men participate in the healing power of the New Being. Otherwise, they would have no being. The self-destructive consequences of estrangement would have destroyed them. But no men are totally healed, not even those who have encountered the healing power as it appears in Jesus as the Christ. Here the concept of salvation drives us to the eschatological symbolism and its interpretation. It drives us to the symbol of cosmic healing and to the question of the relation of the eternal to the temporal with respect to the future.

What, then, is the peculiar character of the healing through the New Being in Jesus as the Christ? If he is accepted as the Savior, what does salvation through him mean? The answer cannot be that there is no saving power apart from him but that he is the ultimate criterion of every healing and saving process. We said before that even those who have encountered him are only fragmentarily healed. But now we must say that in him the healing quality is complete and unlimited. The Christian remains in the state of relativity with respect to salvation; the New Being in the Christ transcends every relativity in its quality and power of healing. It is just this that makes him the Christ. Therefore, wherever there is saving power in mankind, it must be judged by the saving power in Jesus as the Christ.

2. THE CHRIST AS THE SAVIOR (MEDIATOR, REDEEMER)

Traditional theology distinguished between the person and the work of Christ. The person was the subject matter of Christology; the work was the subject matter of soteriology. This scheme was abandoned in the concept of the New Being in Jesus as the Christ and its universal significance. It was a rather unsatisfactory and theologically dangerous scheme. It created the impression that the person of the Christ is a reality in itself without relation to what has made him the Christ, namely, the New Being—the power of healing and salvation—in him. The correlation with those for whom he became the Christ is missing in this double, but separate, description of person and work. On the other hand, the work was understood as an act of the person who was the Christ, whether or not he had performed his work. This is one of the reasons for the understanding of the atonement as a kind of priestly technique undertaken for the purpose of salvation—even if this technique includes self-sacrifice. Many of these semimechanistic mistakes in the doctrine of salvation could have been avoided if the principle had been accepted that the being of the Christ is his work and that his work is his being, namely, the New Being which is his being. With the help of this principle, we can dispose of the traditional division of the work of Christ into his prophetic, priestly, and kingly work, whereby his office as prophet covers his words, his office as priest his self-sacrifice, his office as king the ruling over world and church. Under certain circumstances such distinctions are homiletically and liturgically useful, but they have no systematic value. The significance of Jesus as the Christ is his being; and the prophetic, priestly, and royal elements in it are immediate consequences of his being (besides several others), but they are not special "offices" connected with his "work." Jesus as the

Christ is the Savior through the universal significance of his being as the New Being.

Besides the term "Savior" (*soter*), the term "Mediator" is also applied to the Christ. The term has deep roots in the history of religion. Religions of both the non-historical and the historical types use the idea of mediator-gods to bridge the gap between men and the highest gods who have become increasingly transcendent and abstract. The religious consciousness, the state of being concerned unconditionally, must affirm both the unconditional transcendence of its god and the concreteness which makes possible an encounter with him. The mediator-gods have grown out of this tension. They made the transcendent divine approachable for men, and they elevated man toward the transcendent divine. They united in themselves the infinity of the transcendent divinity and the finitude of men.

But this is only the one element in the idea of the Mediator; the other is his function to reunite what is estranged. He is Mediator in so far as he is supposed to reconcile. He represents God toward man and man toward God. Both elements of the idea of the mediator have been applied to Jesus as the Christ. In his face we see the face of God, and in him we experience the reconciling will of God; in both respects he is the Mediator.

The term "Mediator" is not without theological difficulty. It can suggest that the Mediator is a third reality on which both God and men are dependent for revelation and reconciliation. This, however, is untenable, from both the christological and the soteriological point of view. A third kind of being between God and man would be a half-god. Exactly this was rejected in the Arian heresy. In Christ the eternal God-Man unity has appeared under the conditions of existence. The Mediator is not a half-god. This was the first great anti-heretical decision of Christianity, namely, that he is not a third reality between God and man.

This must be emphasized even more strongly with respect to soteriology. If the Mediator is a third reality between God and man, God is dependent upon him for his saving activity. He needs someone in order to make himself manifest, and—even more misleading—he needs someone in order to be reconciled. This leads to the type of doctrine of the atonement according to which God is the one who must be reconciled. But the message of Christianity is that God, who is eternally reconciled, wants us to be reconciled to him. God reveals himself to us and reconciles us to him through the Mediator. God is always the one who acts, and the Mediator is the one through whom he acts. If this is understood, the term "Mediator" can be used; if not, it should be dropped.

A similar semantic difficulty is connected with the term "Redeemer" (as well as "redemption"). The word, derived from *redemere* ("buying back"), introduces the connotation of someone who has men in his power—namely, Satan—to whom a ransom price must be paid for their liberation. This imagery is not strong in the ordinary use of the term "Redeemer," but it has not altogether disappeared. The symbolism of man's liberation from demonic powers plays a great role in the traditional doctrines of atonement. Therefore, it is quite justifiable to apply the term "Redeemer" to Jesus as the Christ. However, the word has a dangerous semantic connotation, similar to that of the word "mediator." It can create an image of someone who must pay a price to the anti-divine powers before God is able to liberate man from the bondage of guilt and punishment. This leads to the discussion of the doctrine of atonement and its several types.

3. DOCTRINES OF ATONEMENT

The doctrine of atonement is the description of the effect of the New Being in Jesus as the Christ on those who are grasped by it in their state of estrangement. This definition points to two sides of the process of atonement, to that in the manifestation of the New Being which has an atoning effect and to that which happens to man under the atoning effect. In the sense of this definition, atonement is always both a divine act and a human reaction. The divine act overcomes the estrangement between God and man in so far as it is a matter of human guilt. In atonement, human guilt is removed as a factor which separates man from God. But this divine act is effective only if man reacts and accepts the removal of guilt between God and man, namely, the divine offer of reconciliation in spite of guilt. Atonement therefore necessarily has an objective and a subjective element.

The subjective element makes the process of atonement partly dependent on man's possibilities of reaction. In this way a moment of indefiniteness is introduced into the doctrine of atonement. This is why the church instinctively refused to state the doctrine of atonement in definite dogmatic terms, as in the case of the christological dogma. This also opened the way for the development of different types of the doctrine of atonement. All of them were admitted in the church, and each of them has a special strength and a special weakness.

These types can be distinguished as predominantly objective, predominantly subjective, and stages between the two. This itself corresponds to the objective-subjective character of the processes of atonement. Objective in a radical sense is the doctrine developed by Origen, namely, that the liberation of man from the bondage of guilt and self-destruction became possible by a deal between God, Satan, and Christ in which Satan was betrayed. Satan received power over Christ; but he did not have the right to exercise this power over someone who was innocent. His power over Christ and those who are with Christ was therefore broken. This construction of Origen is based on a group of biblical passages in which the victory of the Christ over the demonic powers is expressed. This line of thought has recently been re-emphasized under the title *Christus Victor* (Aulen). It seems that, in this formulation of the doctrine of atonement, any relation to man is completely lacking. A cosmic drama—almost a comedy in the case of Origen—happens above man's head; and the report of the drama provides man with the certainty that he is liberated from the demonic power. But this is not the real meaning of the objective type. In Paul's triumphant verses about the victory of the love of God in Christ over all the demonic powers, it is the experience of the love of God which precedes the application of this experience to a symbolism involving demonic powers—consequently, the symbol of the victory of Christ over the demons. Without the experience of the conquest of existential estrangement, the *Christus Victor* symbol never could have arisen either in Paul or in Origen.

But this general consideration is not sufficient to evaluate the objective theory of atonement. One must examine the concrete symbols themselves. The betrayal of Satan has a profound metaphysical dimension. It points to the truth that the negative lives from the positive, which it distorts. If it completely overcame the positive, it would destroy itself. Satan can never keep the Christ, because the Christ represents the positive in existence by representing the New Being. The betrayal of Satan is a widespread motif in the history of religion, because Satan, the principle of the negative, has no independent reality.

The world into which Christianity came was filled with fear of the demonic powers considered as both the sources of evil and the tools of punishment (a mythical expression of the self-destructive character of existential estrangement). These demonic powers prevent the soul from being reunited with God. They keep one in bondage and under the control of existential self-destruction. The message of Christianity was one of liberation from this demonic fear. And the process of atonement is that of liberation. But the liberation from the fear of destructive and punishing power is possible only if something happens, not only objectively but also subjectively. The subjective element is the experienced impact of the inner power of him who is externally subdued by the demonic powers. Without the experience of the power of the New Being in Jesus as the Christ, his atoning subjection to the forces of existence would not have been able to overcome demonic fear.

It is therefore not astonishing that Abélard developed a theory by stressing the subjective side of the processes of atonement, though without denying the objective side. The liberating impression made upon men by the picture of Christ the Crucified is the impression of his self-surrendering love. This love awakens in man the answering love which is certain that, in God, love, not wrath, is the last word. But this is not sufficient to take away the anxiety about guilt and the feeling of having to undergo punishment. The violated justice cannot be reestablished by the message of the divine love alone. For love becomes weakness and sentimentality if it does not include justice. The message of a divine love which neglects the message of divine justice cannot give man a good conscience. One can refer here to depth psychology, with its practice of making the patient go through the torment of existential insight into his being (though not in a realistic or legalistic sense) before promising any healing. In so far as the predominantly subjective description of the process of atonement misses this point, it could not be accepted as adequate by Christian theology.

The fact that Anselm did justice to this psychological situation is the main reason why his doctrine was the most effective one, at least in Western Christianity. In its form it belongs to the predominantly objective type. It starts with the tension in God between his wrath and his love and shows that the work of Christ makes it possible for God to exercise mercy without violating the demands of justice. The infinite worth of the suffering of the Christ gives satisfaction to God and makes unnecessary the punishment of man for the infinite weight of his sin.

Only the God-Man could do this, because, as man, he could suffer and, as God, he did not have to suffer for his own sins. For the believing Christian, this means that his consciousness of guilt is affirmed in its unconditional character. At the same time he feels the inescapability of that punishment which is nevertheless taken over by the infinite depth and value of the suffering of the Christ. Whenever he prays that God may forgive his sins because of the innocent suffering and death of the Christ, he accepts both the demand that he himself suffer infinite punishment and the message that he is released from guilt and punishment by the substitutional suffering of the Christ.

This point gave the Anselmian doctrine its strong psychological effect and kept it alive in spite of its dated legalistic terminology and its quantitative measuring of sin and punishment. The discovery of an often deeply hidden guilt feeling has given us a new key for an explanation of the tremendous effect of the Anselmian theory on personal piety, hymns, liturgies, and much of Christian teaching and preaching. A system of symbols which gives the individual the courage to accept himself in spite of his awareness that he is unacceptable has every chance to be accepted itself.

A criticism of the theory has already been made in connection with our discussion of the titles "Mediator" and "Redeemer." We have also referred critically to the legalistic and quantitative categories that Anselm uses in his description of the objective side of the atonement. We must add an even more basic criticism—made by Thomas Aquinas— that the subjective side of the atoning process is not present at all. Thomas adds the idea of the participation of the Christian in what happens to the "head" of the Christian body, the Christ. The replacement of the concept of substitution by the concept of participation seems to be a way to a more adequate doctrine of atonement, in which the objective and the subjective sides are balanced.

4. PRINCIPLES OF THE DOCTRINE OF ATONEMENT

The implicit and partly explicit criticisms of the basic types of the doctrine of atonement make it possible to give principles which should determine the further development of the doctrine of atonement—or what may even replace it in future theology.

The first and all-decisive principle is that the atoning processes are created by God and God alone. This implies that God, in the removal of the guilt and punishment which stand between him and man, is not dependent on the Christ but that the Christ, as the bearer of the New Being, mediates the reconciling act of God to man.

The second principle for a doctrine of atonement is that there are no conflicts in God between his reconciling love and his retributive justice. The justice of God is not a special act of punishment calculated according to the guilt of the sinner. But the justice of God is the act through which he lets the self-destructive consequences of existential estrangement go their way. He cannot remove them because they belong to the structure of being itself and God would cease to be God— the only thing which is impossible for him—if he removed these consequences. Above all, he would cease to be love, for justice is the structural form of love without which it would be sheer sentimentality. The exercise of justice is the working of his love, resisting and breaking what is against love. Therefore, there can be no conflict in God between love and justice.

The third principle for a doctrine of atonement is that the divine removal of guilt and punishment is not an act of overlooking the reality and depth of existential estrangement. Such thinking is often found in liberal humanism and is supported by them by comparing the divine and human forgiveness in the Lord's Prayer. This comparison, like all comparisons between divine and human things (e.g., in the parables of Jesus), is valid to a point but is wrong if driven beyond it. While the point of analogy is obvious (community in spite of trespasses), the difference must be clearly stated. In all human relations he who forgives is himself guilty, not only generally, but in the concrete situation in which he forgives. Human forgiveness should always be mutual even if it is not outspokenly acknowledged. But God represents the order of being which is violated by reparation from God; his forgiveness is no private matter.

The fourth principle for a doctrine of atonement is that God's atoning activity must be understood as his participation in existential estrangement and its self-destructive consequences. He cannot remove these consequences; they are implied in his justice. But he can take them upon himself by participating in them and transforming them for those who participate in his participation. Here we are in the very heart of the doctrine of atonement and of God's acting with man and his world. The problem, of course, is: What does it mean that God takes the suffering of the world upon himself by participating in existential estrangement? The first answer is that it is a highly symbolic kind of speaking, but a speaking which is not strange to the biblical writers. God's "patience," God's "repentance" (change of mind), God's "toil with human sin," "God not sparing his Son," and other expressions of this type disclose a freedom for concreteness in speaking of God's living reactions to the world of which theology is naturally afraid. If we try to say more than the symbolic assertion that "God takes the suffering of the world upon himself," we must add the statement that this suffering does not contradict God's eternal blessedness and its basis, namely, God's eternal "aseity," his being by himself and therefore beyond freedom and destiny. On the other hand, we must refer to what has been said in the sections on God as living, namely, the element of non-being which is eternally conquered in the divine life. This element of non-being, seen from inside, is the suffering that God takes upon himself by participating in existential estrangement or the state of unconquered negativity. Here the doctrine of the living God and the doctrine of atonement coincide.

The fifth principle of a doctrine of atonement is that in the Cross of the Christ the divine participation in existential estrangement becomes manifest. Once more it must be stressed that it is a basic distortion of the doctrine of atonement if, instead of saying "becomes manifest," one says "becomes possible." On the other hand, "becomes manifest" does not mean only "becomes known." Manifestations are effective expressions, not only communications. Something happens through a manifestation which has effects and consequences. The Cross of the Christ is a manifestation in this sense. It is a manifestation by being actualization. It is not the only actualization, but it is the central one, the criterion of all other manifestations of God's participation in the suffering of the world. The guilty conscience which looks at the Cross sees God's atoning act *in* it and *through* it, namely his taking the destructive consequences of estrangement upon himself. The liturgical language which derives consolation in guilt and death from the "merit" of Christ, from his "precious blood," and his "innocent suffering" points to him in whom God's atoning act is manifest. But neither the liturgical language nor the uneasy conscience differentiates in the act of faith between the terms "in the Cross" and "through the Cross." Theology *must* make a differentiation (because of the first of these principles) between the two. The Cross is not the cause but the effective manifestation of God's taking the consequences of human guilt upon himslf. And, since the atoning process includes the subjective side, namely, the experience of man that God is eternally reconciled, one can say that atonement is actualized through the Cross of the Christ. This partly justifies a theology which makes God's atoning act dependent on the "merit" of the Christ.

The sixth principle of a doctrine of atonement is that through participation in the New Being, which is the being of Jesus as the Christ, men also participate in the manifestation of the atoning act of God. They participate in the suffering of God who takes the consequences of existential estrangement upon himself, or, to say it succinctly, they participate in the suffering of the Christ. From this follows an evaluation of the term "substitutional suffering." It is a rather unfortunate term and should not be used in theology. God participates in the suffering of existential estrangement, but his suffering is not a substitute for the suffering of the creature. Neither is the suffering of the Christ a substitute for the suffering of man. But the suffering of God, universally and in the Christ, is the power which overcomes creaturely self-destruction by participation and transformation. Not substitution, but free participation, is the character of the divine suffering. And, conversely, not having a theoretical knowledge of the divine participation, but participation in the divine participation, accepting it and being transformed by it—that is the threefold character of the state of salvation.

In the light of the principle of participation and on the basis of the doctrine of atonement, we must now consider this threefold character of salvation in which the effect of the divine atoning act upon men is expressed: participation, acceptance, transformation (in classical terminology, Regeneration, Justification, Santification).

5. The Threefold Character of Salvation

a) *Salvation as participation in the New Being (Regeneration).*—The saving power of the New Being in Jesus as the Christ is dependent on man's participation in it. The power of the New Being must lay hold of him who is still in bondage to the old being. The description of the psychological and spiritual processes in which this happens belongs to the part of *Systematic Theology* which is called "Life and the Spirit"

(Vol. III). At this point, however, it is not the human reaction which is the subject matter under consideration. It is the objective side, the relation of the New Being to those who are grasped by it. This relation can be called "grasping and drawing into itself," producing the state which Paul called "being *in* Christ."

The classical terms for this state are "New Birth," "Regeneration," "being a new creature." Obviously, the characteristics of the New Being are the opposite of those of estrangement, namely, faith instead of unbelief, surrender instead of *hubris,* love instead of concupiscence. According to the usual terminology, these are only subjective processes, the work of the divine Spirit in the individual soul. But this is not the only way in which pre–New Testament and New Testament sources use the term "Regeneration." Regeneration is a state of things universally. It is the new state of things, the new eon, which the Christ brought; the individual "enters it," and in so doing he himself participates in it and is reborn through participation. The objective reality of the New Being precedes subjective participation in it. The message of conversion is, first, the message of a new reality to which one is asked to turn; in the light of it, one is to move away from the old reality, the state of existential estrangement in which one has lived. Regeneration (and conversion), understood in this way, have little in common with the attempt to create emotional reactions in appealing to an individual in his subjectivity. Regeneration is the state of having been drawn into the new reality manifest in Jesus as the Christ. The subjective consequences are fragmentary and ambiguous and not the basis for claiming participation in the Christ. But the faith which accepts Jesus as the bearer of the New Being is this basis. This leads to the second relation which the New Being has to those who are grasped by it.

b) Salvation as acceptance of the New Being (Justification).—The priority of Justification or Regeneration was discussed in the process of salvation. The Lutheran emphasis is upon Justification; the pietistic and methodistic upon Regeneration. A decision between them is dependent partly on the way one defines the terms but partly also on different religious experiences. Regeneration can be defined as actual transformation. If this is done, it is identical with Sanctification and must definitely be put in the second place. The meaning of the atoning act of God is that man's salvation is not dependent on the state of his development. But Regeneration can also be defined as in this system, namely, as participation in the New Being, in its objective power, however fragmentary this may be. If defined in this way, Regeneration precedes Justification; for Justification presupposes faith, the state of being grasped by the divine presence. Faith, justifying faith, is not a human act, although it happens in man; faith is the work of the divine Spirit, the power which creates the New Being, in the Christ, in individuals, in the church. It was a pitfall in Protestant theology when Melanchthon placed the reception of the divine Spirit after the act of faith. In this moment faith became an intellectual work of man, made possible without participation in the New Being. For these reasons, one should put Regeneration, defined in the sense of participation in the New Being, before Justification.

Justification brings the element of "in spite of" into the process of salvation. It is the immediate consequence of the doctrine of atonement, and it is the heart and center of salvation. Like Regeneration, Justification is first an objective event and then a subjective reception. Justification in the objective sense is the eternal act of God by which he accepts as not estranged those who are indeed estranged from him by guilt and the act by which he takes them into the unity with him which is manifest in the New Being in Christ. Justification literally means "making just," namely, making man that which he essentially is and from which he is estranged. If used in this sense, the word would be identical with Sanctification. But the Pauline doctrine of Justification by grace through faith has given the word a meaning which makes it the opposite pole of Sanctification. It is an act of God which is in no way dependent on man, an act in which he accepts him who is unacceptable. In the paradoxical formula, *simul peccator, simul justus,* which is the core of the Lutheran revolution, the in-spite-of character is decisive for the whole Christian message as the salvation from despair about one's guilt. It is actually the only way to overcome the anxiety of guilt; it enables man to look away from himself and his state of estrangement and self-destruction to the justifying act of God. He who looks at himself and tries to measure his relation to God by his achievements increases his estrangement and the anxiety of guilt and despair. In the discussion of the failure of self-salvation, we prepared the ground for this statement. For Luther, the absence of any human contribution was so important that Melanchthon formulated the "forensic" doctrine of Justification. He compared God with a judge who releases a guilty one in spite of his guilt, simply because he decides to do so. But this is a way of stating a doctrine of Justification which leaves out of consideration the subjective side, namely, the acceptance. Indeed, there is nothing in man which enables God to accept him. But man must accept just this. He must accept that he is accepted; he must accept acceptance. And the question is how this is possible in spite of the guilt which makes him hostile to God. The traditional answer is "Because of Christ!" This answer has been interpreted in the preceding sections. It means that one is drawn into the power of the New Being in Christ, which makes faith possible; that it is the state of unity between God and man, no matter how fragmentarily realized. Accepting that one is accepted is the paradox of salvation without which there would be no salvation but only despair.

A word must be said about the expression "Justification by grace through faith." It is often used in the abbreviated form of "Justification by faith." But this is extremely misleading, for it gives the impression that faith is an act of man by which he merits Justification. This is a total and disastrous distortion of the doctrine of Justification. The cause is God alone (by grace), but the faith that one is accepted is the channel through which grace is mediated to man (through faith). The *articulus stantis et cadentis ecclesiae* must be kept clear, even in the formulation of Justification by grace through faith.

c) *Salvation as transformation by the New Being (Sanctification)*.— As a divine act, Regeneration and Justification are one. Both describe the reunion of what is estranged. Regeneration as the actual reunion, Justification as the paradoxical character of this reunion, both as accepting the unacceptable. Sanctification is distinguished from both of them as a process is distinguished from the event in which it is initiated. The sharp distinction in the Reformation between "Sanctification" and "Justification" is not rooted in the original meaning of the words. "Justification" literally means "making just," and, on the other hand, "Sanctification" *can* mean "being received into the community of the *sancti*," namely, into the community of those who are grasped by the power of the New Being. The differentiation between the terms is not due to their literal meaning but to events of church history, such as the resurgence of Paulinism in the Reformation.

Sanctification is the process in which the power of the New Being transforms personality and community, inside and outside the church. Both the individual Christian and the church, both the religious and the secular realm, are objects of the sanctifying work of the divine Spirit, who is the actuality of the New Being. But these considerations transcend the frame of this part of *Systematic Theology*. They belong to what will be discussed in the fourth and fifth parts of the system— "Life and the Spirit," "History and the Kingdom of God."

This concludes the third part, "Existence and the Christ." Actually, however, neither the doctrine of man nor the doctrine of the Christ is brought to an end within this part. Man is not only determined by essential goodness and by existential estrangement; he is also determined by the ambiguities of life and history. Without an analysis of these characteristics of his being, everything so far remains abstract. Also, the Christ is not an isolated event which happened "once upon a time"; he is the power of the New Being preparing his decisive manifestation in Jesus as the Christ in all preceding history and actualizing himself as the Christ in all subsequent history. Our statement that the Christ is not the Christ without the church makes the doctrines of the Spirit and of the Kingdom integral parts of the christological work. Only external expediency justifies the separation of the parts. It is the hope that some of the problems which remain open in this part will find answers in the subsequent parts.

INDEX

INDEX